Organize Your Life for God

FOUNDATIONS:

Book One

Author:

Kelli Newman

Contents

About the Author: Kelli Newman 5
Part 1: Establish a Firm Foundation 15
    Part 1 Introduction 17
    Week 1: Foundation 21
    Week 2: Humility 29
    Week 3: Strength/Weakness 33
    Week 4: Love 39
    Week 5: Joy 47
    Week 6: Peace 51
    Week 7: Patience 57
    Week 8: Kindness 65
    Week 9: Gentleness 69
    Week 10: Faithfulness 75
    Week 11: Self Control 83
Part 2: Let Go of Control 91
    Part 2: Introduction 93
    Week 12: Where, How, What? 95
Part 3: Establish Self-Awareness 99
    Part 3: Introduction 101
    Week 13: How Well Do You Know Yourself? 103
Part 4: Re-Organize Your Life Priorities 109
    Part 4: Introduction 11
    Week 14: How Well Are You Prioritizing Your Life? 115
    Week 15: Faith 117

Week 16: Prayer Life..121

Week 17: Prioritizing God's Will..125

Week 18: Self-Discipline..127

Week 19: Serving Others..129

Part 5: Get Rid of the Chaos!...*133*

Introduction Part 5..135

Week 20: Jealousy / Discontentment..137

Week 21: Anxiety/ Depression...143

Week 22: Worry/Fear...147

Week 23: Selfishness...151

Week 24: Self-hate/ insecurities...155

Week 25: People Pleasing..161

Week 26: Pride...167

Week 27: Unhealthy habits..177

Week 28: Toxic people...201

Week 29: Old baggage...183

Week 30: Look for Changes in Your Life!..191

Take Aways...*193*

Moving Forward...*197*

Acknowledgements...*199*

References..*201*

Organizing Your Life God's Way: From Chaos to Control..*203*

Future Books in this Series..*205*

Follow the Author: Social Media Profiles...*207*

About the Author: Kelli Newman

My Story, His Glory

> *"My Grace is sufficient for you, for my power is made perfect in weakness." "Therefore, I will boast all the more gladly about my weaknesses, so that Christ's power may rest on me. That is why, for Christ's sake, I delight in weakness, in insults, in hardships, in persecutions, in difficulties. For when I am weak, then I am strong." 2 Cor 12: 9-10 (NIV).*

I choose to believe that our trials make us stronger! I have been sick for nineteen years, a little over half of my life. When I was a junior in high school in 2006, I started having symptoms that resembled having a stroke. I was slurring my words, my smile was drooping, and I was having trouble chewing and swallowing food. A couple of months later, I received the diagnosis of Myasthenia Gravis (MG).

Most of you probably have never even heard of MG as it is very rare. Myasthenia Gravis is an autoimmune disease that interrupts the connection of nerves and voluntary muscles (skeletal muscles that you have control over moving). The muscles are essentially attacked by the body's own immune system causing damage to the receptors for the nerves. Receptors are where muscles and nerves meet, and how the brain signals muscles to move. The damage causes severe weakness for someone with MG. The weakness can affect any skeletal or voluntary muscle in the body. Muscles used to move or perform tasks become weak, especially with prolonged repetitive use. The treatments for MG consist of medications that suppress the immune system, and a procedure called Plasmapheresis (Plasma exchange) for short.

A Plasma exchange simply separates plasma (the clear portion of your blood) from red blood cells. Then, once separated, the plasma is removed. Plasma is the portion of the blood in which antibodies are carried throughout the body to fight infection. The removal of the plasma prevents the antibodies from having a chance to attack the muscle/nerve receptors. The plasma is replaced by albumin during the procedure to prevent fluid imbalances.

So, here I was at age seventeen, in competitive dance, entering my senior year of high school, and I received this life-altering diagnosis of MG. My world was literally turned upside down. Prior to my diagnosis, I had been thinking about a profession in the medical field. After receiving such wonderful care from a few special nurses, who still take care of me to this day, I decided to become a nurse. I wanted to be able to help others just like they had helped me. Before graduating college, the Dean of Nursing tried to convince me not to become a nurse. She said it would be too difficult with my diagnosis. To her dismay, I

Graduated Suma Cum Laude in 2011 with a 3.89 grade point average. It is because I went to nursing school that I learned how to take care of myself and my disease. I may not have been writing this book today if it weren't for me fulfilling this calling, and God helping me through it.

About 1 year later in August 2012, I met the love of my life, William. Will met my entire family on our very first date. Some might have said he was a little crazy, but I thought of it as a bold move. Someone willing to meet the entire family on the first date was definitely not afraid of commitment. We were having dinner for my sister's birthday, and he asked if I would like to go out with him that night. At that point I countered with, "My family is having dinner for my sister's birthday, but you are more than welcome to join us." To my surprise, he actually said yes! It was history from there! We all fell in love with him that night. I have no doubt that God placed him in my life for a reason. About six months later, even after learning what being with me entailed, he asked me to marry him. Of course, I said yes! We were married in September of 2013.

After three wonderful years, a lot of prayer, preparation, and faith, God blessed us with our beautiful and perfect baby girl. We named her Sadie Faith. Her middle name is Faith because we knew a test of our faith was approaching, and after my sister Faith whom I will introduce later. God took care of us both, and for that I will always be so thankful! It was very risky for me to have children. We did not know how pregnancy would affect my health, as there was not much research on pregnancy and Myasthenia Gravis. We were taking a huge risk. But we are so thankful that we had faith that God would provide for us! Sadie is such a huge blessing in our lives.

A couple of years after having Sadie, in 2018, I was the sickest I had ever been. I found myself in the ICU with difficulty breathing. I could not even sit up without help. When I would try to call the nurse from my room, she could barely even understand me because my speech was so slurred. I was not able to eat or drink without choking. The doctor ordered an MRI, because he wanted to rule out any other possible causes for my severe weakness. When I got up from the stretcher to move to the MRI table, I went to lay back and I literally just fell backward onto the table. The abdominal muscle strength that I once had was just gone. It was just such a helpless feeling. There are no words for the weakness and fear I felt at that moment. I just cried through the entire MRI. I remember laying there, trying to be still through the tears, just praying that God would give me my strength back and bring me back home to my family. I felt so alone in that moment, but I knew God was with me. I'm still here today, so clearly God still has plans for me. I just didn't understand "the why's" while I was in that moment.

So, to summarize my story, over the past eighteen years I have been fighting for my life while working and striving to be a good wife and mom. I have been on nine different immunosuppressive and chemo medications, had over two-hundred-thirty plasma exchanges, and many hospital stays. In 2020, when covid hit, I was forced to stay home and not work for a while. Not working helped with my symptoms tremendously. Will, seeing me feeling so well for the first time in a long time, encouraged me to stay home. In 2021 I came to the realization that I could not help others if I did not take care of myself first. So, in July of 2022, we decided that I would stay at home permanently and pursue filing for disability. I believe this was all part of God's plan. He took care of me when I was diagnosed, and placed people in my life so strategically. God gave me such loving parents who took care of my needs, and He sent Will to be by my side at such a time as this.

God continues to provide for us daily. When the time came for us to make the decision for me to stay home, we had faith and trusted that God would provide. He most certainly did! He provided Will with an amazing company to work for, Smith's Plumbing. They care about our well-being as a family and have been such a huge blessing to us in so many ways. I can never repay them enough! God provided support for our family through our church ministry 'Love One More'. He provided me with the ability to stay at home to focus on raising our daughter! He provided me with more energy so that I could be a better wife and mother! God really, truly showed us His love. "And my God will meet all your needs according to the riches of His glory in Christ Jesus." Phil 4:19 (NIV).

Where God guides, He provides! "The Lord will guide you always; He will satisfy your needs." Isiah 58:11. Sometimes when God calls us to do something it makes absolutely no sense. But when we follow where He leads, rest assured, He always pulls us through. What we have learned over the years is that God requires wholehearted commitment. After I started staying home, about six months to be exact, God laid on our hearts, heavily, that we needed to be faithful in tithing. After all, everything we have and every blessing we have been given is from our Father. We were scared to make this monetary adjustment, because the amount just didn't make sense financially. We didn't know how it was going to work. Even-so, we were feeling God call us to be obedient! We went over our finances and rearranged some things. We made our tithe the first thing that comes out of every check and placed it at the top of our list of importance. To our surprise, we have not had a single time since, where we were in need that God hasn't provided. What a blessing! Amen?

Once again, God placed something else on our hearts a few short months later. I remember it like it was yesterday. Will and I were on our way home from a trip to the beach, just the two of us. I was feeling better than I had in years. We had talked about this subject a few years prior but never followed through. There I was sitting there in the car, thinking about how I would love to be able to have another child. I started thinking about fostering children. Now that my health was better, I felt that I would be able to physically handle raising another child. Then a song came on the radio about loving a child like he or she was your own. Will looked at me, and he said, "How do you feel about pursuing fostering?" It was such a huge God moment for us! Literally, no one could have planted those thoughts, in that order, it was the Holy Spirit. I said yes! We were so sure that God was calling us to foster that we filled out the application on our drive home. We started classes a couple months later, and in January 2023 we became an approved foster home.

We accepted our first placement in April just a couple days after Easter. We welcomed a group of siblings ages one, three, and five into our home. They turned our world upside down, in a good way of course! Things were so crazy going from a family of three to six overnight. There quite literally are no words for the amount of joy and love we felt while having them in our home. They were with us for eight months, April to December of 2023. In December, they went to live with family in New York. Over those eight months, we celebrated birthdays, took them on vacations, worked through some tough feelings, discovered a new meaning to "Thanksgiving", and we celebrated Christmas early just so we could see the joy on their faces one last time before they left our home. But most importantly, we were able to teach them about Jesus and how much He loves them. Amen!? They began to fight about who would get to say prayers, and no longer said, "God is not real." If that is not fulfillment, I don't know what is! We still get to talk to them weekly and are beyond thankful that they had an aunt that loved them enough to take them into her home as her own.

When we started fostering, we wanted to be able to bless kiddos with the love of Jesus, but as it turns out they blessed us immeasurably. We were able to experience what it was like to be the hands and feet of Jesus. I can't even imagine not having said yes to God's calling that day in the car. We were meant to be a home that provides safety and healing by means of the only person capable, Jesus Christ! Each and every person and home have a purpose and a calling to fulfill. It may not be fostering, but if we call ourselves a Child of God, then it is our duty to pursue God's purpose and calling for our lives! Even though I am no longer able to help others as a nurse, I am still fulfilling a purpose, God's purpose. His purpose is greater than anything that I could ever desire for myself. "Many are the plans in a person's heart, but it is the Lord's purpose that prevails." Prv 19:21 (NIV).

In the year and a half that it took for me to write this book and self-publish, we had nine beautiful, precious children in and out of our home. I read through the entire Bible for the first time (thanks to The Daily Grace Company's Chronological Story of Scripture, *Eden to Eternity*). All the while, I was still getting treatments for my autoimmune disease. I'm not saying all of this to make myself look "good." I'm saying this because when you are doing something God is calling you to do, YOU WILL NOT FAIL! There is literally no risk involved for doing what God calls you to do, because the reward is far greater than we can ever imagine! What do you have to lose? God provides your every need!

We cannot resist God's Calling! "Trust in the Lord with all your heart and lean not on your own understanding; in all your ways submit to Him, and He will make your paths straight." Prv 3:5-6 (NIV). This was the first verse I ever learned, and it has been such an influence in my life. Nothing happens by coincidence. God orchestrates every piece of our story. Our life circumstances sometimes test our Faith, but we must continue to pray and minister with confidence and Trust that God will guide us to fulfill His purpose. At the very least, we can share our story, so that God can use it to reach others.

God's power is literally made perfect in our weakness. Don't you think that it shows courage when we are not fearful of showing our weaknesses and vulnerabilities? God wants to use our weaknesses and allow them to make us stronger, to build our trust in him, and to show others our faith. If God can save me, then He can do the same for you! The Bible tells us to be Glad in our weaknesses, insults, hardships, persecutions, and difficulties! We must trust Him in the good, and the bad times. As a testimony to Him, He wants us to share our story with others. When we share our story, people can see just how mighty He is. Like the Matthew West song says:

"My story, Your Glory; My Pain Your Purpose;
My Mess, Your Message; One life One Mission;

One Reason why I'm Living'; All for You not for me!"

That should be our daily prayer! We just have to do one thing, Allow God to Guide and provide! He is trying to write our story, and trust me, His version is better! In the first book of this series, *Foundations*, it is my hope that you will in fact be able to understand the path to organizing your life the way God designed! He wants to transform your life from chaos to control. Emphasis on His control, not ours! There are five steps to organizing your life for God: Develop a firm foundation, let go of control, establish self-awareness, re-organize life priorities, and get rid of the chaos! Once you have achieved these five steps, other areas of your life can be transformed as well! I have organized this study into five parts (thirty-weekly devotions) so that you can spend time really focusing on each step. Evaluating where you are in your life and allowing God to take control will help you fulfill your God given purpose! Everyone goes through trials and feelings of weakness! Allowing God to use our weaknesses for good is hard, but so rewarding! There is a purpose in every aspect of life! What is yours?

Part 1: Establish a Firm Foundation

Part 1 Introduction

I don't quit, Something I tell myself daily! Perseverance is key! Life is not easy, but no matter what happens to us, we must not quit! We have to tell ourselves constantly, "I will not allow myself to give up." Notice, I did not say, "I will not accept help." There is a difference. We must identify and recognize when we need help and be willing to accept it. In our lifetime, we will experience struggles of great magnitude "far beyond our ability to endure." When this occurs, God wants us to realize that we need Him and rely on Him rather than ourselves. 2 Cor 1:8-9 (NIV). God puts certain people in our lives at certain times for a reason! We should not be so prideful that we cannot accept help. We must remember "Who" is strengthening and helping us! God is! Is 41:10-13 (NIV). He CAN do it! He Does do it! He always has, and He always will! We must not give up! We must not lose hope! We must not lose sight of the reason why we are here! We must not lose sight of God's purpose for our lives. We should live our life in accordance with His purpose and plans, because He will always prevail. He will never give up on us, so why should we give up on ourselves?

God puts us here for a reason! He has a goal and a plan for everything and everyone. God allows us to go through trials to make us more equipped and resilient. Thus, we must in turn share our story with others. Most importantly, we must get through life in order to share how God carried us through it. When we share our story, others should see God. Someone else is struggling with the same things we are daily, and they need to hear our voices to pull them through, to be their Light. God wants to us be a beacon of hope, which brings me to why I'm writing this book. As I sit here in my hospital bed, I am currently dealing with some health issues, not the first and probably not the last. I have to tell myself, "I do NOT quit, and I will NOT quit." Being 'sick' is not new to me! I know that I am a tough, strong, and determined woman. But I also know that God gives me my strength every single day and His power is made perfect in my weakness! 2 Cor 12: 9-10 (NIV). This is what I want to teach my child: How to be strong in the Lord even when we are weak. In the end, our strength comes from Him, not us. Our strength does not come from ourselves or any other thing or person. God is the giver of all of our strength. He is the giver of everything that we have: Life, love, happiness, faith, strength. He and only He can take it away.

While I mention that God gives me my strength, I must also mention that this concept did not come overnight for me. I grew up in a home that taught me the love of Jesus from a very young age. I attended church, learned about God's word, memorized verses, and watched my parents and how they handled life's struggles. I understood what being saved meant, and that all people are sinners. I was taught that a loving God, sent His only Son here on Earth to die for us so that our sins could be atoned for once and for all. I chose to believe that Jesus died for me, so that I could be forgiven. But it wasn't until my adulthood that I really truly understood what a relationship with Jesus meant. It meant that my life should be organized around Jesus. He is our foundation! Our life as believers should imitate the life Jesus modeled for us all those years ago. He portrayed the truest form of Faith, Hope and Love. He was the only person ever capable of perfection. What a blessing to be Loved by Jesus! He should be at the forefront of our life, which means Jesus should be more important than anything else!

This series is based on the Biblical truth that: If we develop a firm foundation in Christ, every other aspect of our lives will follow suit. A firm foundation in Christ will enable us to endure the test and trials of life! Mt 7:24-27 (NIV). If we have read the Word and have committed to follow God's direction, then certain things should be evident in our lives. Fruitfulness is the proof that we in fact are living our lives for Jesus and are being transformed. Christ was the perfect example for us to model.

Spiritual growth takes time and commitment. It does not happen overnight. But, if we fill ourselves with the Word, we will begin to embody the fruits ourselves! Our foundation consists of understanding forgiveness, humility, strengths/weaknesses, love, joy, peace, patience, kindness, gentleness, faithfulness, and self-control.

Week 1: Foundation

What does the Bible have to say about forgiveness?

Some people hold on to the hope of reconciliation until their dying days while others grasp onto resentment and anger. One day, they realize it is too late to convince someone that they are sorry, or to late to forgive someone for the past. As Christians, we understand what forgiveness really means. It means we not only choose to forgive someone for what they did, but we let go of our "right," or so we may feel, to get even or make them pay for what they did. The truth is, it was never our right in the first place. We are not to judge. There are times when we may think, "There is not anything in this world that can fix what has happened to me." Well, that is correct, there is not a "thing" or "person" in this world that can. But see, God, He is different! When He is in our heart, He can do things that no other person or thing can. He changes the way we think, the way we feel, and the way that we act. Jesus gave us the most perfect gift of forgiveness. We do not deserve to be forgiven, yet he does it, time and time again. His forgiveness is limitless when we genuinely repent. Lk 17:3-4 (NIV). There is no cap on the number of times we can mess up and be forgiven by God. If we repent truthfully, He will forgive, and so should we!

This is how we should forgive others. I know it is easier said than done. But, if there is someone that has broken your heart time and time again, it is not too late for them, and it is not too late for you. There is, however, a point in life where you can no longer look that person in the eyes and say, "I'm sorry," or "I forgive you." Trust me, it is much harder to find healing when things are left unresolved. So don't wait, tell them to their face. Be the person that takes the first step. You never know, maybe that person has been trying to find the words for years. Be the reason they find peace. See it on their face. As long as we are still here, there is still time. I say this with love, and I hope it helps you too. Sometimes I need to hear something, but I don't want to. Sometimes it just takes a stranger's words to move me.

    These are the verses that speak to me the most regarding God's forgiveness and our own responsibility to forgive others. Reading these verses truly helps me to understand the true depth of what forgiveness really means. I have written a summary of each passage, but as a rule of thumb, I recommend you read each passage on your own first and then my summary after. Sometimes, when someone else tells you what a passage means to them, you are taking God's opportunity away to speak to you through His Word. That is not my intention! The general understanding of a passage is the same, but God may be laying something on your heart that I did not include in my summary! So please, take your time, read the Word first, and process the passages on your own as well! When you are done, take some time to pray and ask God to give you a forgiving heart. Forgiveness is a gift that we need to share with others!

Mt 6: 12, 15 (NIV). God's forgiveness requires us to forgive others. Is there anyone in your life that you need to make amends with?

Mt 7:1-5 (NIV). You will be judged by God based on how you judge others. First, judge yourself before pointing fingers at others. Do not judge, instead discern. At the same time, do not give others what they will not appreciate or take care of. Self-protection is ok. Judgment attacks, Discernment protects. Is there anyone that you are "attacking" with judgement? Have you addressed your own heart and motives? Are you protecting yourself?

Mt 7:6 (NIV). "Do not give dogs what is sacred; do not throw your pearls to pigs. If you do, they may trample them under their feet and turn and tear you to pieces." Forgiveness should not compromise self-preservation. You can forgive someone, but also not allow them to continue to hurt you. Forgiveness is not a sacrifice of your well-being; it is a sacrifice of your right to get "even." We are allowed to set boundaries for people who do not recognize and appreciate our value in Christ. We should use discernment in self-preservation. Don't let others blow out your candle!

Lk 6:37 (NIV). Do not judge or condemn and you will not be judged or condemned. How does it feel knowing that God judges us how we judge others? Is this enough to change your mindset?

Lk 11:4 (NIV). The Lord's prayer, "Forgive us our sins, for we also forgive everyone who sins against us…" Have we truly forgiven 'everyone' that has ever wronged us? Or is there something we have chosen not to resolve because it just hurts too much?

Lk 17:3-4 (NIV). "If your brother or sister sins against you, rebuke them; and if they repent, forgive them. Even if they sin against you seven times in a day and seven times come back to you saying, 'I repent,' you must forgive them." Forgiveness is Limitless! There is no cap on the number of times we can be forgiven or forgive someone else, only a restraint on the time we have to do it! We are not promised tomorrow! Jesus says if they repent, we must forgive… times infinity! However, there should be self-preservation boundaries. Healing cannot happen without forgiveness. Reconciliation is the goal. Who in your life does this apply to? How can you guard your heart, while still offering forgiveness? Go to God and ask Him.

Rom 10:9 (NIV). "If you declare with your mouth, 'Jesus is Lord,' and believe in your heart that God raised Him from the dead, you will be saved." Have you asked God for forgiveness? It all starts with this. You must understand the magnitude of forgiveness that our Lord has offered. He wants us to accept it and forgive ourselves also. What do you need to ask forgiveness for? What do you need to forgive yourself for?

Rom 12:19-20 (NIV). Overcome evil with good and leave the avenging to God. You may confront those who have wronged you, but do it with the intent of helping them, not for personal gain or revenge. Is there anyone you feel you left things beyond repair with? Have you talked to the person that you need to reconcile with? Speak to them with love and sincerity, and they will see that you mean no harm. They will let their guard down if you do. Just be patient, give them space if they need it. God's timing is everything.

Eph 6:12 (NIV). "For the struggle is not against flesh and blood, but against the rulers, against the authorities, against the powers of this dark world and against the spiritual forces of evil in the heavenly realms." People are not the true enemy, Satan is. Who are you treating like the enemy?

1 Pt 3:8-13 (NIV). We should "repay evil with blessing," so that we may be in turn blessed. Even if we suffer for what is right, we are blessed. Isn't that beautiful? There is beauty even in suffering. God's mercy and grace always prevails. We should always choose what is right even if it is radical and not viewed as popular in our society today. God's spiritual rewards are far greater than any human gain. Have you been disheartened by others' actions or decisions? Can you take a stand for Christ and choose to forgive them, pray for them, and wish blessing on that person?

1 Jn 1:9-10 (NIV). We must confess our sins. God is faithful, just, and forgiving. If we do not confess that we are sinners, it is as if we don't trust God and we are living without His Word in our hearts. What do you need to lay at God's feet? What are you tempted by that you need to give to God and remove from your life? There is no person too broken for God's forgiveness and love! He knows our hearts!

Week 2: Humility

Humility is such a powerful tool! It is honest judgment of ourselves. Humility means actively seeking to be less self-serving. When you humble yourself, it is an outward expression of your hunger to be like Christ. We can have a healthy image of ourselves, yet still not put ourselves above others. God created us equal. We are all uniquely gifted. Our special talents, when combined with others' can accomplish great things. We should not judge others; in fact, we should be keeping a watchful eye on ourselves and our own selfish thoughts and actions.

No one is perfect, but we are perfectly made! Amen! God does not make mistakes! Humility does not mean that we cannot accept compliments or recognition. However, we should do it in a way that is not prideful! God is proud of us when we are faithfully living our life and on mission to win people for Him. He is proud of us when we help others, and when we put others before ourselves and our own selfish desires. Jesus was the perfect image of humility. We have a lot to live up to! This week, really think about your thoughts and actions. Three times a day for a week I want you to recognize opportunities to put others before yourself! You will be surprised how much enjoyment this will bring you!

Ps 139:13-16 (NIV). God created us. We are "fearfully and wonderfully made." God's works are wonderful. He does not make mistakes. He wrote our story in His Book before we were ever formed. What are you thankful for that God has gifted you with? Spend some time in prayer thanking God for the gifts He has given you and for the opportunity to use them!

Prv 11:2 (NIV). When we are prideful, we are a disgrace to God, but when we humble ourselves, we prove to be wise. Are there any things you have been openly too prideful about? You can still choose to believe in yourself yet stay humble. List some things in your life that you feel proud of or maybe you brag too much about. Then instead of telling others, tell God how thankful you are for those things!

Lk 6:38 (NIV). Give to others and it will be returned to you. Whether it is a sacrifice of your time, money, skill, or some other resource that you have to offer, consciously and intentionally seek to help someone, somewhere! List some ways you can help others around you.

Rom 12:3 (NIV). Do not think of yourself more highly than anyone else, instead judge yourself, keeping in mind what God sees in you. Tell yourself, "I am not perfect, but I am perfectly made!" Do you unintentionally put yourself higher than anyone? If so, pray for God to help you lift that person up! God wants us to encourage one another not judge one another! We are all equally loved by God!

Phil 2:3-8 (NIV). Our actions should not be for selfish gain. Instead, we should value others interests before our own. We should humble ourselves. Who are you 'living' life for? If it is for anyone other than God, then your motives are in the wrong place! Seek to please God by putting others first! Pray for God to place His desires on your heart! How can you choose to humble yourself daily?

Week 3: Strength/Weakness

Strength and weakness are both things that God can use for good! I believe true strength is a product of enduring those weak moments. When we trust God in those moments, He gives us the strength to endure. This is perhaps one of the most difficult things for most people to understand! We are not in control! Because when we are in that moment of weakness, it can feel so helpless and vulnerable. But our faith in God allows us to cling to His promises. He is a beacon of hope. The moments when I have been at my weakest physically, are the times when I have felt closest to God. You see, when we don't have a relationship with Christ, we may feel like God has abandoned us. That hope in Christ is missing, and thus we feel as if we are not going to survive the struggle. But as a Christian, we know that we are under Gods protection, and even if God allows us to suffer, there is a purpose that we don't see. When we depend on Christ, our weaknesses become strengths, and our relationship with Christ grows. Thus, weakness produces strength!

I still remember being diagnosed with MG and the feelings of fear that it brought. I remember sitting in the ICU bed wondering if the treatment was going to start working, or if I was going to be able to breathe easier and eat normal food again. I remember the feeling of worry. Would we be able to find a new medication that would work before I crashed again? All these times, even though that fear and anxiety crept in, I remember feeling God's presence. I was surrounded by prayer, my family and friends, and the feeling of peace. I knew that my life was in God's hands no matter what happened! Each and every time I am in these weak moments, I always remember and am always thankful for God's part in my recovery. My disease is not curable, except by God. He will protect me, for He has conquered the world. Jn 16:33 (NIV). So why worry?!

In the past several years, I have really felt a sense of healing. I am able to recognize that in all that I have been through, there is a purpose. My relationship with Christ has grown stronger and I am able to see now that God has given me a story to tell. My story can help others going through similar struggles in life. Even though I have been struggling to survive with this disease for nineteen years, over half of my lifetime, I have joy knowing that God is using my weakness and my story to help give others Hope for strength in Christ as well. These are the verses that really speak to me in my times of weakness! Read these verses and spend some time with God. List your strengths and weaknesses. Pray for God to use these verses to help you and maybe eventually others in times of struggle.

Josh 1:9 (NIV). God commands us to be strong, courageous, unafraid, and not discouraged! God is always with us. What are you afraid of? Pray and leave those fears at God's feet! Trust Him!

Ps 31:24 (NIV). If Christ is within you, you can be strong and confident! Who have you placed your hope in? Do you have confidence in yourself? Pray that God convicts you to have confidence in Him! Believe in Him. God is your strength! Allow Him to work in you and through you! What are you confident about?

Ps 73:26 (NIV). Even if our bodies fail us, God's spirit is within us and the Holy Spirit is our strength. He gives us fulfillment. What weakness is holding you back? What do you need to allow God to help you fulfill?

Is 40:29-31 (NIV). "He gives strength to the weary and increases the power of the weak." Hope in the Lord renews our strength. Hope requires patience, trust, faith, and confidence in the Lord's timing. We must wait for Him. God is above time; He is not controlled by it! His timing is perfect! What do you hope for? Pray that if it is God's plan, it will be given to you!

2 Cor12: 9-10 (NIV). His Grace is enough. His power is made perfect in our weakness. Christ's Power becomes ours when we have faith. Because of this, we should take pride in "weakness, insults, hardships, persecutions, and difficulties." When we are weak, He makes us strong! What weakness/trial are you going to praise God for? How have you grown spiritually because of it? Allow your struggle to bring you closer to the Lord!

Phil 4:13 (NIV). "I can do all this through Him who gives me strength." What things have you been putting off because you don't have the strength to do it alone? What are you afraid of?

2 Thess 3:3 (NIV). The Lord strengthens and protects us. Pray for the Lord to protect you in seeking His mission! What weaknesses do you have that you can use as strengths? Thank the Lord for helping you see the gifts He has given you.

Jas 1:12 (NIV). When we persevere in trials and persecution for the Love of Christ, we will be blessed. Look for the good that comes out of the hard times. What good has come out of your hard times? How has God blessed you?

Week 4: Love

The first verse that comes to mind when I think of love is Jn 3:16-17. Christ suffered and died for us! What a powerful image of what love is. We do not deserve the love that He has given us. This is the intensity of love we should have for everyone. The Bible says that if we don't love our brother and sister, we do not love God. 1 Jn 4:20 (NIV). What a statement! God truly loves us unconditionally. Likewise, there should be no conditions on our love for others. We should love regardless of whether we feel respected or loved ourselves. The idea is that if we show others God's love, they will want to understand Him more. We should be loving people with a goal of winning them for the Kingdom of God!

Often it is hard to portray this level of love and commitment because we are just human, and our emotions and pride get in the way. But if we are faithfully giving love in the face of betrayal, it will literally eat at that person, until they eventually give in. Some people have never experienced love, and to be honest it scares them to feel this type of connection with someone. For example, children who are neglected often push people away when they experience true love for the first time. It makes them feel vulnerable when someone tries to connect. They don't always recognize it, but they are afraid of trusting someone, because other people in their lives have repeatedly abandoned them in times of need. Sometimes they stop trying to seek love all together because previous attempts have been futile. Sometimes, they act out to get attention and love because that is the only way they have been able to get it in the past.

When my Husband and I started fostering, we had a hard time wrapping our head around the reasoning behind how one of our kiddos was behaving and pushing us away. It is so hard to repair that feeling of abandonment. Love is such a necessity in our growth and development. Love is important in all phases of life: As a child, as an adult, and as a newborn Christian. Jesus portrayed a whole new level of love when He died on the cross for us. The most important way to gain understanding on love is from reading the word of God. Spend time reading these verses, and praying for God to open your heart to others like Jesus does!

Mt 5:44 (NIV). "Love your enemies and pray for those who persecute you." Who do you need to pray for?

Lk 10:27 (NIV). We are to love God with all our heart, soul, strength, and mind. God also commands us to love others as we do ourselves. Does God truly have all of your love and focus? What do you need to let go of so that you can commit your all to God? Love is more than just a word; it is an action! How can you show God you love Him? How can you show others God's love?

Jn 3:16-17 (NIV). "For God so loved the world that He gave His one and only Son that whoever believes in Him shall not perish but have eternal life. For God did not send His Son into the world to condemn the world, but to save the world through Him." God loves us, and He does not want to beat us down! What are you beating yourself down about? Do you want to be saved? Allow God to love and forgive you!

Rom 8:28 (NIV). God is working in all things, good and bad. God helps those who are called and are fulfilling His purpose. His children are those who seek and hear His calling and act. Are you fulfilling His purpose? God wants what is best for you, because He loves you! Let Him guide you! Where have you seen God use disaster or devastation for good?

1 Cor 13:2-3 (NIV). If we have wisdom and everything valuable life has to offer, but do not have love, we have nothing. Who do you need to be showing more love to in your life?

1 Cor 13:4-7 (NIV). "Love is patient, love is kind. It does not envy, it does not boast, it is not proud. It does not dishonor others, it is not self-seeking, it is not easily angered, it keeps no record of wrongs. Love does not delight in evil but rejoices with the truth. It always protects, always trusts, always hopes, always perseveres." Are you following this definition of love that is so clearly laid out for us in God's word? What areas do you need to work on? What areas are your strengths when it comes to love?

1 Cor 13:13 (NIV). Faith, hope, and love are three very highly valuable theological virtues. The one which God values the most is Love. Love is mentioned over 300 times in the Bible. Are you taking advantage of God's love? It is free! We don't have to earn it or deserve it! All we have to do is accept it and share it with others! Have you accepted it? Do you need to share it with someone. Who in your life needs to experience God's love?

1 Cor 16:14 (NIV). "Do everything in love!" What things do you not like doing? This week, I want you to do these things with love! I know it may be hard but do them for Jesus! Be joyful about it!

1 Jn 2:15-17 (NIV). If you love the world and the things of the world, you do not love God. The world will pass, but those who do God's will live eternally. What things in this world are you putting before God? Re-arrange your priorities so that God takes priority over the things you spend time, money, and resources on!

1 Jn 3:18 (NIV). We should not love with words, but with actions and truth. How can you show God with your actions that you Love Him?

1 Jn 4:8 (NIV). "Whoever does not love, does not know God, because God is love." Do you have hate in your heart? Pray for God to remove it from you! Rebuke it daily and any time the thought enters your mind!! Satan is the enemy not people!

1 Jn 4:21 (NIV). Loving God means loving one another. Who do you need to tell that you love them today? How can you follow with actions? Make them believe it!

Week 5: Joy

"Joy is not necessarily the absence of suffering, it is the presence of God"-Sam Storms

I absolutely love this definition of Joy! I think it truly embodies the holy, pleasing, presence of our Lord. He brings such a huge sense of happiness in our life, when we choose Him. We have to choose to believe that God designed the world to be good! We have to see beauty in the good and the bad circumstances in our lives. We are blessed no matter what happens to us! When we truly have God in our heart, we see life differently. I have to admit, this does not just come easy for me. I tend to catch myself complaining when things are not going the way I think they should. But I am only human, just as you. I think that choosing Joy is harder than choosing bitterness. When we are going through life it is so easy for us to think, woe is me, why is God allowing this to happen!

Self-pity is a perfectly normal reaction to trials. But, when we get to this thought in our daily walk, we must pray for God to show us how we can find the good in our situation. What is something that came out of the darkest part of your story that is good? Choose to think about those blessings, and praise God for them. Let the growth renew your joy! You can even ask God how you can turn your situation around or get yourself out of it. The last thing we need to do is allow Satan to steal our Joy. He will use all sorts of schemes to make us miserable. We just have to rebuke those negative thoughts and replace them with the beautiful Word of God! Amen!? God can turn your thoughts around if you let Him! The Bible plays such a huge part in finding Joy in the day to day! Meditate on these verses. Spend some time thanking God for the wonderful life He has given you, and the spirit of Joy that he has placed within you!

Ps 33:21 (NIV). Our hearts rejoice because we can trust in the Lord. What is your favorite name for God? Why is it your favorite? Lift His name in praise! Thank Him for giving you Joy!

Ps 71:23 (NIV). We can be joyful because God has delivered us. What has God delivered you from? How can you thank God for His deliverance?

Ps 118:24 (NIV). The Lord has given us this day so let us rejoice and be glad in it! Today is a good day because we are alive! What were your thoughts this morning when you got out of bed? This week, start the day by praising God instead of complaining! What can God use you to do today?

Prv 17:22 (NIV). "A cheerful heart is good medicine, but a crushed spirit dries up the bones." What negative thoughts do you have that you need to get rid of! How can you transform those thoughts into positive/encouraging thoughts?

Rom 15:13 (NIV). "May the God of hope fill you with joy and peace as you trust in Him, so that you overflow with hope by the power of the Holy Spirit." Would you say you are a joyful person to be around? Does your attitude rub off on others around you? Do you allow others' attitudes to affect yours? Where does your joy come from?

Jas1:2-4 (NIV). We should "consider it pure joy when we face trials," because we know that the "testing of our faith produces perseverance." Perseverance matures and completes us and produces wisdom. Are you joyful in your trials? What areas do you lack maturity or wisdom?

Week 6: Peace

Sometimes I can't stop my thoughts from rolling with worry at night. It is hard to find a sense of peace in this chaotic world. We are so bogged down by work, school, afternoon schedules, friendships, relationships, media, and news. The list of worries can be never ending. I tend to feel like I have peace when everything is planned and goes accordingly. But what happens when the plan changes? What then? I can't help but think, "Backup plan anyone?!" This is the mindset I am fighting daily! I have to remind myself, there is peace in living this life the way God has planned for me! We must let go of the things we cannot control!

So how do we find the will power to just stop and "smell the roses?" Well, if we think it will just happen on its own, we are never going to really be able to enjoy this wonderful life that God has given us. Our life is a blessing. Each and every day we have the satisfaction of knowing that God is moving and working. He literally never stops working! He wants us to have peace and clarity of mind. But we have to choose to purposely strive to remove the negative thoughts from our mind. No one can quiet your mind like God. There is an unexplainable peace that comes over you when you worship Him! Sometimes I get chills during worship or prayer. I believe that this is the Holy Spirit just letting me know there is no reason to worry or fear!

God's presence is everywhere around us! We see it everywhere in creation. Every day we need to remind ourselves that it is a good day, because God created it to be so! I have peace knowing that Christ has experienced all the things that I am experiencing. He understands and can feel my happiness, pain, love, anxiety, and sorrow. He not only knows my thoughts, but He feels my every emotion! It brings me such a sense of peace. God cares for me, and He cares for you! I hope you never feel like there is no one to turn to. Even on your darkest of days, you are never alone! These verses really hit home for me when I am anxious or worried! I hope they give you a sense of what God's peace is truly like. You have to believe and trust that God has everything under control!

Is 26:12 (NIV). God establishes our peace. All that we have accomplished is because of Him. Do you trust God? You must trust God to have peace. What do you need to trust God with?

Mt 5:9 (NIV). "Blessed are the peacemakers, for they will be called children of God." Is there someone you need to make peace with? Pray for God to give you the words to say to that person!

Mt 11:28 (NIV). If you are burdened or weary, go to God and He will give you rest. What burden do you need to lay at God's feet?

Jn 14:27 (NIV). God gives us peace! We should not worry or be afraid. What are you worrying about? What are your fears? What has worrying or being fearful done to help your situation? Pray and ask God to help you! Let go of the worry and fear, because He is already answering your prayers!

Jn 16:33 (NIV). We can have peace knowing that "In this world we will have trouble." But Jesus has "overcome the world." List the biggest, most impossible thing that you are trying to overcome or accomplish. Now pray for that, knowing that God can do all things! He has no limitations!

Phil 4:6-7 (NIV). We should not be anxious about anything. Instead, we should go to God in prayer, thanks, and request of our needs. God's unexplainable peace will "guard your hearts and your minds." What are you anxious about? Maybe you don't even know! BUT God does. Pray for peace of mind!

Jas 3:18 (NIV). If we plant peace, we will harvest righteousness. God values those who try to create peace and contentment! It is not easy sometimes, but it will help us become more like Christ! Where do you need to plant peace? Where do you need to be the "better person" and let go of a disagreement! How can you use that opportunity to show someone the power of God's peace?

1 Pt 5:7 (NIV). "Cast all our anxiety on Him because He cares for you." List a time when God cared for you in a time of need.

Week 7: Patience

Patience is another virtue that is hard for most of us! Or at least it is for me! We are living in a culture that says that we should have instant gratification. Society says if we don't, then something is wrong with the system, when it's actually the other way around. Our world is the broken system. It has been broken for a very long time! When we wait patiently and work to live out God's will, the outcome is sweeter than anything we could ever imagine. See, God literally has all the time in the world to work with. He created the timeline. It is His.

God is the author. We must wait for him to finish writing out our story. Sometimes we don't understand it because we don't see the big picture. When you are putting a puzzle together, you usually have an image to copy. However, with our image, God is holding the copy in His hands! We must wait for Him to put the pieces together to see the finished project! If we allow this to happen, we become a beautiful masterpiece, intricately designed by God. But just think, if we lose a piece to a puzzle, it cannot be completed. The same things goes when we try to follow our own path and desires and do not seek God's guidance. A piece of us is missing from God's puzzle. He is actually the one patiently waiting on us to commit our life to Him. He needs us for an even bigger puzzle that we are completely unaware of! We just have to trust the Creator!

There have been several times throughout my life when I wondered if God was ever going to answer to my prayers. When I was a little girl I prayed for years for a sibling. I was surprised, when at age twelve, I was told I was going to be a big sister. When I was 6 years old, I was saved. From that point forward, I prayed year after year for my dad to come to know Jesus. It wasn't until I was twenty-seven, that He finally felt the Holy Spirit's call and was saved. It was such a beautiful day! Praise God! He is faithful! When I was in my late teens and twenty's, I thought I was never going to find someone that wanted to marry me because I was so sick. Years past, and I met my husband! I knew he was the one from the day I first met him. I know God handpicked Him for me. The wait was so worth it! I thank God every day for bringing Will into my life. When my husband and I started trying to have children, we knew it would be very risky. We were willing to trust God to provide our hearts desires. It took three years, a lot of prayers, patience, and even some disappointment. But, in His timing, God blessed us with the most perfect baby girl. I am so thankful for our little rainbow blessing!

Again and again, God taught us to be patient. Good things come to those who put their hope in Him! Lam 3:25 (NIV). Finally, in my early thirties, after waiting patiently I was finally approved for disability. This was huge! I finally felt like I was providing for our family again after not working for three years. I know I was providing in other ways, but it made me feel so much better to help relieve the burden on my husband. God provided as he always does! With all this being said, God's timing is perfect. He is good, and he wants to use us for good! So be patient and let Him! Why the rush? God gave us this beautiful life! All we have to do is learn to be patient and trust His design! These verses are pretty amazing to think about! Patience is truly something we need to work on daily!

Ex 14:14 (NIV). "The Lord will fight for you; you only need to be still." What battle do you need God to fight for you? Take a moment to be still and pray for the battles that we fight daily and for patience in the victory.

Ps 31:15 (NIV). Our life is in God's hands. List something you are praying or waiting for. Pray for God's perfect timing and will to be done. Pray for visibility, discernment, and awareness regarding your requests. Keep your eyes open! Sometimes God doesn't answer prayers in the way we expect.

Prv 14:29 (NIV). Patient people are understanding, quick-tempered people are foolish. Patience takes time and time allows understanding to develop. Are you patient or quick-tempered? Are you allowing your mind to process and understand what is happening before you react? Are you sharing your feelings in a way that is helpful and understanding of others' feelings?

Prv 15:18 (NIV). Being ill-tempered stirs up conflict, but patience is calming. Do you pursue conflict? Do you instill a sense of calmness? Try taking some deep breaths or reciting a short verse when you begin to feel flustered and inpatient.

Is 30:18 (NIV). God is gracious, compassionate, and just. "Blessed are all who wait for Him!" In the past, how has God blessed you in your wait? Trust that He will again. Pray for God's blessing over your life.

Jer 29:11-13 (NIV). God has big plans for our lives. He will not harm us, and He gives us "hope and a future." He is always there when we call on Him. What plans are you making currently? Take a minute to stop and pray for guidance regarding those plans! Are they aligned with God's desires? Are you rushing God? Are you waiting on Him? Do you need to hit the pause button and re-evaluate your plan? Are your own plans hindering you from fulfilling God's plans?

Acts 1:7 (NIV). "It is not for us to know the times or the dates the Father Has set by His own authority." Only God can see the big picture! Who is in control of your life?

Rom 8:25 (NIV). Hope is waiting patiently for the things we desire or need. We have hope because we know that God provides for us. What do you hope to fulfill during your lifetime? Are you missing any opportunities? God always provides when we are faithful. Sometimes we do not recognize opportunities because we are not paying attention! Who is truly holding you back, yourself or God? You might need to ask yourself, "Is what I'm asking for aligning with God's plans and desires?"

Gal 6:9 (NIV). Never tire in doing the right things! For in God's timing, we will be rewarded if we do not give up. Have you given up on God? God acknowledges our persistence! What do you need to be persistently praying for?

Col 3:12 (NIV). If we are God's people, then we should be clothing ourselves with, "Compassion, kindness, humility, gentleness and patience." Who do you need to be more patient and understanding with?

Jas 5:8 (NIV). "Be patient and stand firm, because the Lord's coming is near." Is your faith strong enough to take action? Do you need to take a stand where you haven't had the courage to do so? We will answer to God, so be sure you have been a pillar for Him!

2 Pt 3:8-9 (NIV). "With the Lord a day is like a thousand years, and a thousand years like a day." He is not slow at fulfilling His Word, only patiently waiting for all to seek Him for forgiveness. He wants no soul to be lost! God is above time! Is He still waiting on you to follow Him? You may have already asked for forgiveness, but have you truly pivoted? Seek Him and follow where He guides. God is patient, but there will come a day when it is too late to be obedient. Where does God want you?

Week 8: Kindness

My Mama always said, "Kill your enemies with kindness." I have never really been the confrontational type. I usually try to avoid arguments at all costs. Sometimes this led to people "taking advantage" or "walking all over me" as you may call it. I never realized I could kindly and respectfully confront others about the way they were treating me. I tire very easily, but I am a hard worker, and I refuse to let people see that I am weak. However, the truth is, I need to rest more frequently than others. It wasn't until my adult life, that I realized being argumentative and standing up for yourself are two very different things. I had to let go of my pride and ask for help or accommodations when I needed them. I learned that unfortunately some people are not kind, or they just simply do not understand what I am going through. What I didn't realize is, almost everyone has something they struggle with. You can't judge a book by its cover, right? Some weaknesses are invisible. People are not superheroes! I am not a superhero!

Over time, I learned that people could change. People don't know what you are going through unless you let your guard down and share your weaknesses. I think it is safe to say that most people are not ill-intentioned. I have to remember that everyone is going through something. Who am I to judge! People can ask for forgiveness, and they may not deserve it, but we are told to give it freely. Forgiveness takes kindness. In fact, a lot of people in this world are in need of kindness. We should be consumed by showing kindness! So consumed, you ask, that we put others needs before our own? Yes, absolutely! How does that work? Because if we do not take care of ourselves, we can't take care of others, right? These are serious questions that I have asked myself. But it wasn't until recently that I realized the truth. When we take care of others, God takes care of us. God always provides what we need, when we need it! So next time you are given a choice to help yourself or help others, remember we should be a cheerful giver! A lot more can be accomplished when we are kind and compassionate to one another. The Bible makes it very clear that we are to be kind!

Prv 11:17 (NIV). Kindness brings personal growth, but cruelty brings self-ruin. Who do you need to work on being more kind to?

Prv 19:17 (NIV). When you show kindness to those in need, you are giving to the Lord. He will repay you for what you have done! Do you have resources that you could use to help others in need?

Prv 31:26 (NIV). We should speak words of "wisdom and faithful instruction." Is there someone you can take "under your wing?" Is there Someone who is going through something that might appreciate or need an act of kindness?

Lk 6:27-36 (NIV). Be kind to everyone, even your enemies. Give and do not expect return. Treat others the way you want to be treated. Who is your enemy? Find something you can do that they will appreciate.

Acts 20:35 (NIV). Work hard and help those who are weak. It is far better to "give than to receive." Who do you know that is struggling with something? Ask them how you can help them. People often need help, but they are just too afraid to ask!

Eph 4:31-32 (NIV). We are to, "Get rid of all bitterness, rage and anger, brawling and slander, along with every form of malice." We should, "Be kind and compassionate to one another, forgiving each other, just as in Christ God forgave you." Do you participate in gossip? How can you get yourself out of a situation and stand up for someone?

Week 9: Gentleness

Gentleness is powerful! It is definitely underestimated. Gentleness is the "underdog." A gentle person is the one you would least expect to be in a position of power. Our society tells us that if you want things in life you have to "take" them. That is not how a Godly leader acts. A Godly leader cares for the people they have authority over. Gentleness is a fruit of the Holy Spirit. If we have the Holy Spirit in us, we should bear fruit of gentleness. There are ways we can work on this particular gift.

First, like all other spiritual gifts, we need to be cultivated by Gods word. Meditation particularly helps me with gentleness. I pray over words I want to speak to someone. I pray that my words may be helpful, true, and not disheartening. It is known that the truth sometimes hurts, but a true friend seeks to help and not criticize. Sometimes gentleness means giving someone some space to cool off. Sometimes it means listening or praying for yourself and that person to find a middle ground. There is a sense of gentleness that the Holy Spirit gives us when we trust in Him! I know that we can all loose our cool at times, but again, we are only human! Sometimes we need to remember that the same rule applies to ourselves. Sometimes we need to be gentle on ourselves. Our words and actions are heavier than we think. If we are not careful, they can cut deep. God is the perfect example of gentleness. It is evident when we read His Word, feel His spirit, and experience His creation.

Prv 15:1 (NIV). "A gentle answer turns away wrath, but a harsh word stirs up anger." How do you respond when someone disagrees with you? Ask yourself, is it worth the argument? Is it worth getting upset? Will it really make a difference?

Prv 15:4 (NIV). "The soothing tongue is a tree of life, but a perverse tongue crushes the spirit." Have you hurt someone by being brutally honest with them? Try explaining to them what you said was out of concern and love for them.

Prv 25:15 (NIV). Patience can persuade, and "a gentle tongue can break a bone." Gentleness is powerful. Who in your life is it hardest for you to be patient and gentle with? Have you prayed for God to help you with that?

Is 40:11 (NIV). God is our Shepard, He "gathers" us, "carries us close to His heart," and "gently leads" us. Are you allowing God to lead you? Where is He leading you?

Mt 5:5 (NIV). "Blessed are the meek, for they will inherit the earth." Who are you? If you think you are powerful there is a problem! Remember God is in control! He created us to be humble, kind, loving, gentle, and submissive to Him. We are here to serve His purpose not our own! Humble yourself before God! Be a gentle soul and it will be recognized! Are you modeling Christ?

Gal 6:1 (NIV). Correct other sinners gently being led by the Holy Spirit. But be sure not to be tempted by them. Who are you around daily that "needs" Jesus in their lives? Are you joining in with them in their sin? How can you gently tell them that you are not going to gossip, slander, or speak ill will of someone because you have chosen to be like Christ? Use that opportunity to talk to them if they ask questions.

Phil 4:5 (NIV). "Let your gentleness be evident to all." If someone were to speak about your character, what would they say?

1 Tm 3:2-3 (NIV). Overseers should be gentle and temperate, not quarrelsome. Would you make a good leader? Are you gentle? Are you quarrelsome?

2 Tm 2:25 (NIV). We should instruct others gently, in hopes that the Holy Spirit will lead them to freedom and repentance through a knowledge of Jesus Christ. Are you instructing others gently when they make a mistake? Are you showing them the gentleness of the Holy Spirit?

1 Pt 3:15-16 (NIV). Always be ready to share your reason for your hope when asked. "But do this with gentleness and respect." Has anyone ever asked you why you have hope? What would you tell them? Can people see the hope within you?

Week 10: Faithfulness

I don't know about you, but I want God to say to me one day, "Well done, good and faithful servant." Mt 25:21 (NIV). God has given us just a little understanding regarding the whole picture that is our life. Our life is a test of our faithfulness. If we cannot be trusted with the gift God has given us, then why do we think He will trust us with the Kingdom of heaven? If we are faithful to God, then our lives should bear the fruit of the Holy spirit. We are weak, but the Holy Spirit has the power to use us to do mighty things. Just think about the "no-bodys" in the Bible that had faith and became Hero's for God: Joseph, Esther, David, Noah, Mary, Abraham and Sarah, Job. Faithfulness wins favor with God; it always has and always will.

There are two very important people in my life that have the name Faith, because of the huge amount of faith it took in God for them to be here! My sister Faith, whom I mentioned, I prayed for many years, is such a blessing in my life! My mother was advised not to have any more children after I was born, because she was diagnosed with Lupus. Twelve years after having me, she unexpectedly became pregnant. What seemed like a very exciting time to me, was a very scary and anxious time for my parents. It was very risky for my mother to have more children. In fact, the doctors told my mom she should terminate her pregnancy. Of course, my mom would have never chosen abortion, being the Christian woman that she is. My dad told her that if she did what the doctor told her to do, she would regret it for the rest of her life. So, they chose to have Faith in God's protection. They named my sister Faith, because of all the Faith it took to have her! Today, she is perfectly healthy and happily married. She graduated from dental hygiene school May of 2024. I could not be more proud of her, and I definitely could not imagine life without her. Some doctor, who didn't know God's plans, tried to convince my mom to act out of fear. Oh, how I'm glad she had Faith instead!

    The second person in my life with the name Faith, was named after my sister. My daughter Sadie Faith is our rainbow baby. I wouldn't have had a child if it weren't for God's protection, and she may not have had a mother. But Will and I believed that if it was God's will for us to conceive, we would. It took three years, which is not that long compared to so many others, but it felt like an eternity. Watching your friends have children, while you are persistently praying for God to give you one baby of your own, is not easy. But God is faithful. He protected us both, and for that I am so very grateful. Sadie Faith has more faith than I could have ever imagined. She will literally stop what she is doing, wherever she is, and pray out loud! When she is done, she moves on as if God has already answered her prayer! Don't I pray for the kind of faith she has! She amazes me daily. She believes with all her little heart and shares God's light with everyone she meets. I could not be prouder of the young lady she is becoming! She shares God's love with so many every day!

Fostering has perhaps been the hardest, most rewarding, leap of faith we have taken yet! Instead of us waiting on God, He was waiting on us to say yes to His calling. We did not know how we were going to afford taking care of more children, or how my health was going to fare. But we felt the Holy Spirit calling us into this ministry, so we jumped in headfirst. Man, oh man did God provide. Every direction we turned we were seeing signs of God's pleasure in the work that we were doing. There were some very hard days, but God sent some great people along the way to help us in our journey.

Recently, we were discussing our presence in our church, and how we were not serving within the walls, like most people. We are tithing of course, but we really have struggled with committing to regular attendance with the kids being sick a lot, my husband working to make up for my not working, and my being sick. We should be there more, I feel guilty for that. I also feel like we are serving God in our home daily, but not in the typical way. Serving should not just happen within the church walls. For us, in this season, it occurs in our home fostering children. We are the church. The church is not just a place! It takes everything we have, and we are committed to that. So, I don't feel like God is judging us for that. All I know is I love my God with all my heart, and my faith has never been stronger. Even when I am not at church I am worshiping and in the Word! Worship is not just about the place, it about belief in Christ and trusting in where He leads! We must be doers! We must reach people, and we must speak His truth! God leads us where He needs us! Be faithful servants!

1 Sm 12:24-25 (NIV). "Fear the Lord, "serve Him faithfully with all your heart", remember what He has provided for you, and turn away from evil. What do you need to turn away from? What has God done for you? What can you do for God?

Ps 91:4 (NIV). God faithfully protects us. Do you feel God's protection? Why or what do you have to be afraid of? It makes Him sad when we don't trust Him!

Prv 2:8 (NIV). God guards the path of those who are faithful. Are you faithfully following where God leads? Where is He leading you? Spend some time in prayer, asking God to make it known to you!

Prv 3:3-4 (NIV). Love and Faithfulness wins favor of God and man. How can you show God you are faithful?

Prv 28:20 (NIV). "A faithful person will be richly blessed, but one eager to get rich will not go unpunished." What is motivating you in life? Who are you worshiping? The things you love are where your heart truly lies. Make sure they are worthy of your love!

Lam 3:22-23 (NIV). We are allowed to live another day because God's love and faithfulness allows us to. How are you using today as an opportunity? Are you wasting God's blessing of life? What opportunities have you been missing?

Mt 7:7-8 (NIV). Ask God for what your heart desires and it will be given to you. What does your heart desire? Pray for God to fulfill that desire if it is His will! Pray fervently!

Mt 25:21 (NIV). If you are faithful with a few things, God will entrust you with more. What has God given you? Have you been faithful with the few things God has entrusted to you? Are you worthy of many? Are you honest and dependable?

Mk 11:24 (NIV). Believe that whatever you have prayed for you have already received, and it will come to fruition. This is true faith! What have you asked God for? Do you have faith and believe with all your heart that He has provided it?

Gal 2:20 (NIV). We have died to ourselves, but now live by faith. Jesus loves us so much, He died for our sins. Are you still living for yourself? Are you living by faith?

Heb 11:11-12 (NIV). Sarah had faith in God's promise to give her a child. Because of her Faith, God was faithful. Abraham and Sarah had more descendants than stars in the sky or sand on the seashore. What impossible thing do you want to see God accomplish through you?

1 Pt 4:19 (NIV). Even if we suffer for doing God's will, we should faithfully continue to do good. What are you suffering for? Pray, thank God, and ask Him to help you endure for His Glory!

Rv 2:10 (NIV). We should be faithful to God "even to the point of death." He will give us eternal life as our reward. Have you been denying God? What beliefs do you stand for? Do not be a conformist! Live counter-culturally! Be a light in the darkness!

Week 11: Self Control

Living a Godly life requires self-control. When we become followers of Christ, we have to strive to be "like" Christ. We have to follow the Bible's instruction on how we should live our lives. How do we know how to live, if we haven't read God's word? It is more than just a book full of wise verses. It is a book full of rich, wonderful stories. Stories of real people, our worlds creation, wisdom, instruction, and warnings. There is so much about character and virtue. We have to learn to control our thoughts, words, and actions. But at the same time, we must acknowledge that we are in control of nothing that happens in life. It is such a hard concept to grasp. One thing is very clear though! Satan is very deceiving, manipulative, and dishonest. We must keep ourselves on guard for his schemes. We should not put ourselves in situations where we will be tempted to do something un-holy. If we find ourselves in a situation unexpectedly, we should have the self-control to get out!

The only person we are pleasing is God! Just remember that. Who cares if we offend someone or loose a friend over our beliefs. We only have one person to answer to. God is our only judge, and he is just. So, we better be careful about what we allow to enter our temple. What goes in, comes out.

I don't know about you, but I would rather people see me as "boring" or a "good girl" who never has fun, than risk my virtue doing things to please people and fit in. I do have to admit it is difficult making friends, especially when they don't have the same beliefs or morals as we do. But again, we have a purpose, and if we aren't careful, we will end up venturing off the path that God wants for our lives. We might even miss the big finale.

Prv 29:11 (NIV). It is wise to be calm, and foolish to lose control in anger. Do you have control of your thoughts, words and actions? How would you rate yourself in this area?

Lk 9:23 (NIV). We must deny ourselves daily in order to follow Christ. What things do you need to deny to follow Jesus? What things are you putting before him? Are you being an example for others?

Rom 8:5-6 (NIV). We should think about what the Holy Spirit desires not what the flesh desires. If we choose to do what the Holy Spirit desires it brings us "life and peace", but the desires of the flesh bring death and destruction. What are you setting yourself up for? Which desires are you following?

Rom 12:1-2 (NIV). Your body should be a holy and pleasing sacrifice to God. If you live counter-culturally, with Biblical understanding and faith, and allow the Holy Spirit to guide you, you will discover God's will and purpose for your life. What are you putting into your body/mind? Is it pleasing to God? What kind of music are you listening to? What TV shows are you watching? What are you eating or drinking? What are you spending your money on? Make sure that they are things that will contribute to good character and God's will.

Eph 6:10-11 (NIV). God has given us power and strength in the Word, so that we may put on His "full armor" and be ready to resist the devil's attacks. Think of something that you can recite when you feel tempted to do something you shouldn't, or when you are feeling defeated. Practice reciting it! Use it as a weapon against Satan when you are under attack!

1 Tm 2:9 (NIV). We should treat our bodies as God's, dressing with decency and modesty. This is not just for women. Ask yourself, "Does what I'm wearing draw attention to me in ways it shouldn't? Is what I'm wearing too revealing? Am I dressing with decency and modesty? Am I causing someone to look at me in a way they shouldn't." Don't help Satan by creating temptation!

2 Tm 1:7-8 (NIV). God did not give us the Holy Spirit so that we may be timid. Instead, he gave us "power, love and self-discipline," so that we may boldly share our testimony. Sometimes, this may even mean that we suffer for the Gospel. What is getting in the way of you sharing your story? Are you afraid of what people will think?

Ti 2:6-8 (NIV). Be so self-controlled, full of integrity, truthful, and virtuous that your rival cannot find anything negative to say about you or hold against you. Have you done anything that could slander Christ's name? When you claim to be a Christian and deliberately sin, people are watching. Are you giving Christ a bad name? What do you need to work on, so that you are a positive, living example of Christ?

Ti 2:11-12 (NIV). Our salvation and grace from Christ allow us to use self-control to say no to the world and live counter-culturally for Him. It's ok to say no! What do you need to say no to that the world has to offer? What do you need to say yes to that Christ has to offer?

Jas 1:19 (NIV). "Everyone should be quick to listen, slow to speak, and slow to become angry." This will produce righteousness. Are you listening before speaking? Are you acting in anger or love? Take time to think about your words and actions! Practice self-control!

1 Pt 4:7 (NIV). End times are near, so we must be alert, sober, and steadfast in prayer. Are you alert? Is there anything keeping you from being clear minded? Are you spending time in prayer? Are you watching for the enemy's attacks? Are you prepared for Christ's return?

2 Pt 1:5-8 (NIV). There is a process for productivity in our walk with Christ. Knowledge of this order will allow us to be effective and productive followers of Christ. Each step leads to the next: "Faith, goodness, knowledge, self-control, perseverance, godliness, mutual affection, and love." Our knowledge and wisdom grow one step at a time starting with our profession of faith. Faith is our reason for living! Are you following these steps? Are you missing any? Where are you at in your walk? Are you developing self-control?

Part 2: Let Go of Control

Part 2: Introduction

God is in Control of Everything!

This is a very hard concept for me to accept. I like to be in control of everything. For my entire life, or my entire young adult life, I felt like I wasn't in control of anything. My health was controlling my life. So, I began doing this thing called "micromanaging." Anyone ever been told they do that?? It is embarrassing sometimes; I am sure I drove people a little crazy! In my head, I told myself I was, "being a leader." It took me some years to recognize and accept that what I was doing was overcompensating for my lack of control. But finally, I began to realize why I felt the need to control everything. There was this subconscious thought I was having that, If I couldn't be in control of my life, then why couldn't I try to control everything and everyone around me? Laughable, I know…But, FINALLY in my adult life I figured out that I am not supposed to be in control of my life, because GOD is.

I am in control of nothing, except for my own actions, and that is OK. I had to let go and let God take the wheel. We cannot and should not try to do everything all on our own. The Bible talks to us about letting go and letting God have control of our lives. Yes, there are things that we can do to help make life easier and less chaotic. God doesn't want us to be foolish, waste time and resources, or do things that will make our lives difficult intentionally. So, it is our job to rely on him for strength, and to use our brain and choose to do things smarter. Relying on Him allows us to live our lives in a Godly way that is Organized and led by Him. Suddenly our lives become significantly less chaotic because He is in control. Who is in control of your life? The first step is commitment! Stop fighting and submit to His will!

Week 12: Where, How, What?

We must ask ourselves: Where, How, and What?

WHERE does God want me to go?

HOW do I Get to where God wants me to go? Is there anything or anyone holding me back?

WHAT must I do to set my life up for God's success?

When we spend time with God, it is like spending time with a friend. We get to know and understand Him better. We get to know what He's like, how He thinks, what He wants, before He even asks. When we spend time with God we begin to understand WHERE He is leading us and WHERE we should be going. Our recognition of His desire becomes clearer. Once we realize where God is leading, we must take the leap of faith and commit ourselves to His mission!

God will provide when we are doing His will. He is the HOW! He is our biggest resource. The Bible is the number one way to set ourselves up for success. But we must read it. You can buy a Bible on Amazon, but if you don't read it, it does nothing for you. Read your Bible, know the Word, study it, meditate on it. Imbed it in your heart and in your brain. Let the Bible, "God's Message," dictate what you do and how you do it. If you don't know the Word of God, then you're not living up to the potential God desires for you. God gave us the ability to learn His Word and he wants us to use wisdom to help others seek him. It is important to ask ourselves, what or who is holding us back from commitment to God: jobs, friends or relationships, social media, denial, feelings of personal betrayal, stubbornness? Whatever it may be, pray and ask God to help you to move past it. When God closes a door, He opens another one. He is the HOW!

Once we recognize where God is calling, and that He is the How, then we should use His resources to set ourselves up for success. Setting ourselves up for God's success means knowing and deciding WHAT we need to achieve His goals. That need can vary drastically depending on the calling, but the message is the same. Use the Word, the resources God has given you, and the Godly people around you. God provides when you are doing His work. "Plans fail for lack of counsel, but with many advisers they succeed." Prv 15: 22 (NIV). If you don't have a church, get involved, get plugged in. Go regularly; make it part of your routine. GO faithfully and keep the Where, How and What on your mind to remind you of your ultimate goal.

Part 3: Establish Self-Awareness

Part 3: Introduction

I realize that I may have a mild case of obsessive-compulsive disorder (OCD). I like things to be a certain way. I feel that when something is not in its rightful place or time, the day doesn't flow smoothly. Things do not happen like they should when there is no order. I feel like my day is chaotic when order, organization, and planning aren't established. It's taken me thirty odd years to realize that it is ok for things to change, and that I need to be flexible! Although OCD may be frustrating, God gave me the gift and desire of wanting to do things perfectly. The gift of being purposeful in what tasks He has given me. If this is your gift and you completely shut it out, it will drive you crazy and run your life. You will not be living up to your full potential.

Use your gift! Now, I'm not saying it is ok to turn the lights off twenty-seven times and go back in the house five times to check to make sure you didn't forget anything! That is not purposefully using your gift! You must ask yourself, "Is this "thing" that I feel like "needs" to happen really making a difference?" If yes, then go for it. But if not, then move on with your day! If we don't think about the things we do and we just act, our lives will be reckless and crazy. There is a time and a place for everything. Having an organized system helps us cope with the craziness of life. It is ok to be prepared!

We are not in control of all things that happen to us. We are however in control of how we react, learn, and handle them. This is one of the biggest concepts that I struggle with understanding myself. Realizing that even though I have a lot of things in my life that are well managed, there are things that are out of my control: health, kids, life circumstances, other peoples' actions. There are so many things in life that are out of our control, but we can still attempt to set ourselves up for success! How? By being organized, having a system, knowing God's Word and applying it. If we know His Word, then we can have the discernment to know what is right or best, and what God would want for our lives. If we aren't familiar with His word, then how do we make wise choices?

    The purpose of this book series is to help you set yourself up to accept and recognize God's blessings and callings when they come. Being self-aware is instrumental to transforming ourselves for Jesus. Notice, I did not say we should be self-centered. These are two very different things. Self-awareness allows us to examine our inner-self, recognize our gifts, and determine which areas of our life need to be more Christ centered. Self-centeredness, the opposite of self-awareness, means putting ourselves first and always focusing on our own personal desires rather than Christ's.

Week 13: How Well Do You Know Yourself?

1. Do I want God to be in control of my life? What areas do I need to let go of control?

2. Am I too busy for God? What time and resources do I have that could be used for God's purposes?

3. What is God's purpose for my life? What can I do to identify His purpose?

4. Where am I gaining knowledge about Christ? Am I applying God's Word in my daily life.

5. What areas of my life do I need to apply wisdom in order to make my life more efficient in fulfilling God's purpose and plans?

6. Where am I spiritually? Where does God want me to be?

7. What is my history and how can I use it to help others?

8. What are my spiritual Gifts?

9. What plans does God have for my life? Do my plans reflect His?

Summary:

We are not in control. God is! He wants to set us up for success. He gives us the tools to do so by means of wisdom and discernment from His Word and other Godly people and influencers in our life. Be self-aware. Identify your spiritual gifts and your history, then use them to help you fulfill God's plans. List your strengths, weaknesses, spiritual gifts, desires, wisdom gained from life struggles. Then be intentional in using them! Allow God to make dreams and goals happen! God can do all things, and He can give us strength to do all things if we choose to allow Him! So let go and let God! Say to yourself "What areas of my life do I need to be more purposeful?" Pray for wisdom over those specific areas in your life.

> *"Confused minds don't take action! Wisdom and understanding must be present before application can take place. God is the foundation for our transformation. Proverbs says that wisdom takes time and investment. It isn't quick decisions or popularity! A lot of people use the excuse, 'I don't have time.' Which really means, 'I choose not to do it.' Quit making excuses and do what you need to do to get the results you want to get." - LaKeisha Michelle*

Find godly people that you can go to for guidance. Let them be a light for you in your transformation. God uses His Word, and He uses His people to transform our lives. Take the first step. Ask yourself these questions and be honest with yourself! It will give you a starting point! Become self-aware!

Part 4: Re-Organize Your Life Priorities

Part 4: Introduction

Who likes containers? I like to think of organizing my life in the same way I use containers to organize things. I like to label them in a way that is simple and self-explanatory. When someone else needs to find something, they shouldn't have to ask where to find it! I realize that life is not "simple," so this can be very difficult to accomplish. Our lives have many different factors that are intricately woven together: Religion, relationships, finances, home, education, businesses, health, emotions, self-awareness/care, leisure, family, jobs, and the list goes on. Each one of these factors can be placed into a "container" of sorts. When life gets crazy things might get out of their "container." This is perfectly normal. Life is messy! However, when we have our life organized around God, we know how, and have the means to put things back together!

With God in our life, everything has a place and a reason! Nothing is by chance! God can help you see the purpose in your life! Let Him guide you. When things don't go as we planned, it might be God's way of telling us that maybe we need to reassess our plans and align them with His. He might be teaching us and molding us into a version of ourselves that is even wiser and stronger! Just remember He is always by our side.

There is beauty in organizing your life for Christ. When life becomes a mess and things start to become confusing and all mixed together, He is holding us and keeping us safe. When our containers get turned upside down, He helps us put our life back together. He uses trials as opportunities to help us clean up our lives and make us stronger. There is a sense of satisfaction and peace when you keep your containers tidy and free from "junk." Containment equals less chaos. I'm not saying you can't mix anything because obviously that's impossible, and not recommended. But for the most part, we should try to keep our lives as clean and simple as possible.

When people look at our lives, they should have a glimpse of the goodness of God! Do not let chaos and discontentment overrun the calmness, happiness, collectiveness, and peacefulness that God has given you! If you want to look even deeper into your life, there are two large containers that contain everything else, a "necessary container" and an "unnecessary container." The unnecessary things in the containers take up space in our lives and can hold us back from doing what God wants us to do. The unnecessary things are different for everyone, but we all have them. They all take up time, space, and resources in our lives that we could be using for God.

We need to get rid of the junk in our containers so that we can fill them with the things we truly need to allow God to use us. Everything in our lives should revolve around Him. If it's not pleasing to God, it needs to get out of our "containers." We carry around a lot of junk in our lives. Who wants to clean it up? If we have a place for everything, then we won't need that junk drawer! I know everyone has one of those. Am I right? God desires for us to live clean, pure, and simplified lives with nothing but the things that are pleasing to Him. When we recognize that we need God and embrace the principles of organizing our lives according to God's way, then we can experience peace and spiritual growth. We begin to see how God's plans and desires are much better than our own!

Week 14: How Well Are You Prioritizing Your Life?

Rate yourself from 1-5 On each of these Principles...

Faith

Prayer

Prioritization of God's will

Cultivation of self-discipline

Serving others

Week 15: Faith

Faith is the fruit of our trust in God. Faith is loyally choosing to believe in God (whom we cannot see) no matter what. When we begin to have trust in God, our faith grows. We must have faith in God's plan and his guidance even when His plan does not make sense to us. We should have faith in the good times and the difficult times. What God tells us to do will not always make sense. It could be the craziest thing you have ever thought about doing, yet your heart (The Holy Spirit) is telling you, "This is what God wants me to do." When you get to this point, it is important to seek spiritual nourishment from God's Word and through prayer. I believe that he gives us discernment through His Word when we need it. His Word is powerful and full of wisdom, truth, and direction.

Our faith is based on God's Word and our own experiences. The more we experience, the more our faith grows. Like the saying goes, "What doesn't kill you makes you stronger." Faith works the same way. When we go through a struggle, our Faith is strengthened, and God's fruit becomes visible within us. The struggle produces fruit in the sense that our faith develops, multiplies, and becomes uncontainable. But God is the vine tender, he prunes the dead vines so the new can grow. Fruitfulness equals SPIRITUAL GROWTH. Your Faith is growing and someday you will have the opportunity to share it with others. Faith is contagious. Our faith in God should be what helps us through day-to-day life, good times and bad. Faith gives us PEACE, a feeling of security knowing that we are in God's hands, and that we are living out His will.

What is your current perspective on life?

1. What are some "good things" happening in your life currently?

2. What are some "not so good/difficult things" going on that are weighing you down?

3. Why do you think God is allowing certain things to happen in your life?

4. What things do you need to let go of and let God take control of?

5. Who can you go to for help or advice?

6. What is God trying to teach you and what good can come out of these experiences?

7. How can you use your experience in "life" to help others?

1. Sometimes when you give others advice, you realize that you knew what to do all along. So, ask yourself, "What would I tell my friend if they were in my situation?"- Follow your own advice. You might be surprised!

Week 16: Prayer Life

Along with faith, prayer is powerful. What is prayer? Prayer is spending time with God. Time with Him, earnestly thanking Him, praising Him for all He does, or seeking His guidance and wisdom. It is that simple. We must be humble, faithful, specific, honest, and vulnerable in our prayers. Prayer is instrumental in organizing our lives because it allows us direct access to God's will. If we do not spend time in prayer with God, how do we expect to know where He is leading us. Prayer is also hugely significant to our spiritual and personal growth. It Is significant and powerful, and we must develop a consistent faithful prayer routine to Grow our relationship with Christ.

We need to be specific in our prayers so that God knows exactly what we are asking. We should seek God's wisdom and guidance in our prayers. For example, I might say, "God please give me wisdom regarding" and fill in the blank. If we don't ask specifically, how will we know when God answers our prayers? An ill-defined prayer gets a vague answer. So, if we don't ask specifically then we may not get the answer we are looking for. Sometimes we still won't get the answer that we're looking for, because God's plans are different than our own. His wisdom is omniscient. He literally knows everything! We must trust that he has and knows what is best for us. We must seek Him and fulfill his work. We must be humble in our prayer life. God is all powerful, mighty, and omniscient. We are not worthy to be in His presence, yet He allows it. For that we should humble ourselves.

We must be honest with God. He already knows every thought we have! So speak! Tell Him your feelings, thoughts, and desires. Prayer gives us peace knowing that God is listening. Spiritual growth happens when we pray for God's wisdom and discernment, believe that He will answer, and wait patiently for His timing.

Evaluate your Prayer Life:

2. Are you setting aside time for prayer in your day to day? How much? When? Make a plan!

3. What things do you need to pray over? Make a list, be specific in your prayers!

4. Are you looking for the answers to your prayers? Are your spiritual eyes open? Sometimes the answer is right in front of you and you just don't recognize it. Pray for wisdom to know when God gives you answers.

5. Are you being patient, or taking matters into your own hands? God's timing is everything.

6. What areas of your life have you cut God out of because you took control and didn't trust where He was leading?

Week 17: Prioritizing God's Will

After faith and prayer life, prioritizing God's will is our next step. "What does prioritizing God's will look like?" you might ask? It means putting God's needs before our own. If we secure our faith, spend time with God in prayer, discover what His will is, and then we do nothing with it, then what does His will produce in our lives? We must align our goals and aspirations with God's purpose and His plans. The Bible says we must take up our cross and follow Christ. Mat 16:24 (NIV). Christ guarantees that God is with us, but He never says it will be easy.

Through prayer and reflection, we can discern God's will and take action. In order to do this, we must let go of our worldly desires and plans and embrace God's plan. We must die to ourselves and be born again in Christ! There are so many things in this world that can become idols if we are not careful: relationships, money, careers, hobbies, addictions, lifestyles, and people. We must make sure that these things are not getting in the way of us prioritizing God's will. If we put God's will into action, we can have peace knowing that His will is our reason for living. He is the way! Prioritizing based on God's desires takes wholehearted commitment and thus creates spiritual growth. Spiritual growth happens when we trust in his perfect plan.

Prioritize God's Will:

1. What things are keeping you from pursuing what God would have you to do?

2. Should you still continue to do these things? What can you do to make changes?

3. Are they necessary or are they unnecessary things in your life?

4. What can you rearrange in your life so that God comes first?

Week 18: Self-Discipline

What is self-discipline? Self-discipline is: overcoming feelings of weakness, abandoning what is wrong, pursuing what is right, and facing and defeating our temptations. How do we cultivate self-discipline? Start by reading God's Word. It is where we get knowledge directly from God about right and wrong! Then, we can start intentionally applying that knowledge! Application of knowledge is wisdom! "By wisdom a house is built, and through understanding it is established; through knowledge its rooms are filled with rare and beautiful treasures." Prv 24:3 (NIV). Wisdom allows us to identify and get rid of those things in our life that are keeping us from doing God's will. Wisdom helps us build a firm foundation and transform it with the holy spirit.

After we've first recognized what those necessary things are, then we can confidently build our foundation. Self-discipline is so important in organizing our lives because it builds accountability, grows spirituality, and strengthens us physically and mentally. If we do not hold ourselves accountable, our goals will not be met. In other words, our goals will not happen. It's that simple. We must put in the work in order to see our lives change. God wants us to be accountable to Him! We don't get to accept God into our lives, expect Him to save us from our sins, and then do nothing in return for Him. That is called "using," or "taking advantage of." God doesn't strike me as someone who tolerates use and abuse! We have to change our lives! Change involves self-discipline. We must learn what His word says in order to know what things we need to change in our lives. Change is not easy or popular. However, nothing worth having comes easy. We must "foster" habits that promote spiritual growth and personal development and throw away "junk" habits that allow Satan to take a strong hold over our lives. Healthy habits foster self-control!

Honesty is the key to self-discipline!

1. .What things are you spending your time and money on?

2. Are your priorities worthy of the time and money you are spending?

3. Are they necessary or are unnecessary?

4. Are your thoughts and actions aligned with God's priorities? Pray for guidance and the ability to use wisdom and discernment when it comes to your thoughts and actions.

Week 19: Serving Others

Once we develop a relationship with Christ through faith/prayer, and follow through with prioritization and self-discipline, we can then take things one step further. Now we can share Christ's love by serving others. Take Action! Serving others means showing love and kindness, even when it is not reciprocated! Our church's mission statement is "Know, Grow, Go." It encourages a mission of servitude! If we do not take action to reach others, then once again, we are not living up to our full potential. We must embrace God's calling to serve others. This looks different for everyone. There are so many areas or outlets to serve. We must anticipate serving. If we are at a loss to find ways to serve, we can pray for God to make clear where he wants us.

Serving can be as simple as just listening to someone going through a hard time, helping someone find discernment/wisdom, donating to a shelter or a charity project, volunteering to serve within the church, or going on local mission trips. Or it can be as drastic as: Fostering children, moving across the world to do mission work, or changing jobs. The most important thing we can do is pray and ask God to lead us where He wants us and go where He calls! Wherever you are, wherever God calls you to go, if you are serving Him, you will find His grace and fulfillment. Blessings will flow.

Have kindness and compassion for others. If you have Christ in your heart, kindness and compassion should flow outward. Put serving others in your "necessary" box! Have a heart for serving! Be like Christ, put others first! Be the hands and feet of Jesus. You can be that one person who makes a difference in someone's life. Serving others brings you a sense of peace and fulfillment! It also fosters spiritual growth. You will begin to see how your faith allows God to use you to reach others. Find a group of people that you can join in mission. Being united in mission allows God all the more power! There is strength in numbers. "For where two or three gather in my name, there I am with them." Mat 18:20 (NIV).

Steps to Find your Niche to Serve

1. What things do you enjoy doing?

2. What do you have experience with? Work, training, hobbies, specialties, trials/experiences?

3. What resources do you have on hand? Personal, or collective? Time, Money, Connections?

4. Who do you feel you could help best? What target population?

5. Set goals! What are your realistic time frames, financial needs/goals, methods of outreach.

Summary

Faith, prayer life, prioritizing God's will, self-discipline, and serving others are the first steps to organizing your life for Jesus. Our lives are in God's hands! We must center our lives around Him. These fundamentals are the core of our foundation. When we establish these first goals, we will begin to see our lives become more purposeful. Things will begin to fall into their place or "containers" and we will begin to see the bigger picture! His way is better than ours. He created the big picture long before we ever existed, and He has our best interest at heart.

God does not want to harm us; He wants to help us! He wants to use us to reach others. We cannot and will not grow if we are not spiritually grounded. Once we allow ourselves to grow spiritually then we will begin to see the other aspects of our lives flourish as well. We must allow the Holy Spirit's "seed" to be planted and take root before spiritual growth can happen. Peace within, and spiritual Growth will happen when we develop our relationship with Christ. It is amazing to see the work God does in our lives when we follow where He leads. He will never stop leading us or fighting for us! He will never stop providing the means and the way! Trust His process and timing!

Part 5: Get Rid of the Chaos!

Introduction Part 5

What is in your Un-necessary Containers?

     Establishing our foundation was the first step to Organizing our lives for Jesus. We fill our necessary containers with the Word of God, so that our life is set up for success. Jesus is our foundation, and He will never fail us. The next step is cleaning out our un-necessary containers. The things of this world that weigh us down, tempt us, and corrupt our God given purpose. These are the things we need to identify and leave behind: Jealousy/ Discontentment, Anxiety/ Depression, Worry, Selfishness, Self-Hate, People Pleasing, Pride, Unhealthy Habits, Toxic People, Old Baggage. Imagine the relief of removing all these burdens we carry and laying them at the feet of Jesus! Give God your burdens, and He will give you rest! Mt 11:28-30 (NIV). Let the word of God give you encouragement and peace. Time to unload the things holding us back and get rid of the chaos they cause in our lives.

Week 20: Jealousy / Discontentment

We live in a culture that tells us how we should act and how we should live our lives. We are encouraged to always seek more than we have. The world does not teach of satisfaction and contentment. The reason that the world is never satisfied is because it is not focused on Jesus! When we don't have Jesus in our lives, we cannot have the satiating feeling of true contentment. The world encourages us to compare ourselves to others, even though God did not make anyone the same. Reality is, the only thing that we should strive to have the same as others is a mission to reach people for Jesus.

Everyone's story is different and unique. God designed us to be that way. He gives us what we need. However, what we need and want may be very different. If our wants align with God's desires, then He will provide a way. Instead of trying to "keep up with the Jones'," we should be striving to focus on what God wants for our lives, spiritual ambition! Spiritual ambition is the desire to seek greater things for the Kingdom of God! Be eager to help others achieve the same thing. Be happy for your friends that are thriving! But also be wary of those who are thriving by loving the world instead of Jesus! There is a difference. Our hearts need to be in the right place. Blessings will come our way when we are content with what the Lord has given us, and we give Him thanks. Praise Him every day, in the good times and bad! God is our very best friend; we should be focusing on pleasing Him above all else! Run the race to win the eternal prize.

Prv 14:30 (NIV). Peace is restoring, envy is destroying. Who are you envious of? Why do you feel that way? Think about what God has given you. Pray for contentment. Thank God for all the many blessings He has given you.

Lk 12:15-21 (NIV). Life is about more than just possessions. Do not be greedy! You cannot take things with you when you leave this Earth. What are you planning on taking with you to heaven? What do think you own that is going to get you into heaven? Do you see the importance of a relationship with Christ? What are you holding onto that is of little importance!

1 Cor 9:24-27 (NIV). Run the race of life to get the eternal prize. Train yourself to think of the eternal victory in Christ, and fight to keep your mind and body spiritually fit for battle. In this way you will not be "disqualified" for the Kingdom of God, but you will be armed and ready to defend it with honor. Are you armed and ready? How do you know? Who are you running the race for? Are you running it with honor?

Gal 5:26 (NIV). If the Holy Spirit is living within us, we should not be conceited. We should not provoke or be jealous of one another. Who can you encourage and build up? Who can you help in their walk with Christ?

Phil 4:19 (NIV). "God will meet all your needs." We should not be discontent in having what we need. Do you have all your needs met? Have you thanked God? What have you been complaining about? Are you discontent? Pray and thank God for meeting your needs!

Heb 13:5 (NIV). Be content with the life you are given, avoid the love of money, and remember that God will never abandon us. Are you hoarding your money? You will get paid again, there is no need to worship money! It is a thing, and it should not come before God. Financial wealth means nothing to God. But how we chose to spend our money does! We should be concerned about using our wealth to help others! Are you using your wealth to help others? Are you making decisions about following God's will based on the financial "how." Are you willing to allow God a chance to intervene? Allow God the chance to provide, you will be amazed!

Jas 3:16 (NIV). Envy and selfish ambition lead to chaos, wickedness, and immorality. Is selfish ambition driving your actions? Is your life chaotic? Do you need to pivot and allow God's desires to help you make decisions? Pray for spiritual ambition!

Week 21: Anxiety/ Depression

Anxiety and depression have no mercy. They creep in, unwanted and uninvited. They take hold of our lives and control us in ways that are debilitating. Fight, flight, and freeze are the words that we have heard describing the way anxiety makes us feel. Anxiety and depression are two of the many schemes that the devil uses to keep us from fulfilling our purpose and God's will. We must recognize that our enemy is the devil and not ourselves. Anxiety and depression are literally attacks by Satan to get us to turn against ourselves. We have to rebuke these thoughts and speak the Word of God over our minds. Rebuke Satan from having an influence over your thoughts. Satan fears God, so if we fill our minds with God's Word, Satan doesn't stand a chance.

I struggle with both anxiety and depression daily. I believe my anxiety stems from my past physical weakness. It has been so severe, that I literally have fear and anxiety about getting sick. I also struggle with thoughts of self-inadequacy because of my physical limitations. I feel guilty for not being able to provide for my family. But over time, I have been able to replace those thoughts of anxiety and depression with the knowledge that God still has a purpose for my life. It just looks a little different than in the past. I am more resilient because I have endured hardships and weaknesses. I can use that resiliency to teach others how to survive, deal with life challenges, and find purpose and thrive even in the chaos. Just remember: God has conquered the world; there is nothing He can't do; and there is no one too far gone. God Can heal your heart, mind, and soul. You just have to trust Him. He is Faithful in all things!

Ps 147:3 (NIV). "He heals the brokenhearted and binds up their wounds." Has you heart ever been broken? Is your spirit defeated? Will you trust God to mend you? Pray and ask God to make you whole and give you peace.

Mat 11:28 (NIV). If you are "weary or burdened" rely on God and He will "give you rest." What is weighing you down? Take the first step and look for what is causing you to feel the way you are feeling. Pray for God to relieve you from that burden!

Lk 12:22, 31 (NIV). Jesus said, (22) "Therefore I tell you, do not worry about your life, what you will eat; or about your body, what you will wear." (31) "But seek His kingdom, and these things will be given to you as well." What are you worrying about? Now, ask yourself, has God ever NOT provided?

Lk 12:25 (NIV). Worrying does not add a single hour to your life. Why are you still worrying? What worries do you need to lay at God's feet? Allow Him to be who He is and do what He does!

1 Pt 5:7 (NIV). "Cast all your anxiety on Him because He cares for you." Are you giving Him a clear mind? If your mind is filled with anxious thoughts, there is no room for His Word and truth! Replace those thoughts with scripture! Memorize the verses that bring your mind peace during the storms! Use them as a weapon against Satan.

Week 22: Worry/Fear

I will always remember the day our daughter Sadie was born. It was such an emotional day for all of us. My water broke unexpectedly, and I had just done a round of plasma exchanges. We wanted to make sure that I would be strong enough and prepared for delivery. My induction day was scheduled, but I went into labor a few days before. God had other plans than my doctor apparently! My water broke very early on a Sunday morning, around four AM. Sadie was born around ten AM. Prior to my delivery I set up meetings with a Neonatal Intensive Care Unit (NICU) physician. My condition is so rare, I wanted to make sure the hospital was prepared for us when the time came. It is so important to be an advocate for yourself, because if you don't, no one else is going to do it for you! Not only was it risky for me to have a child, but there were also risks involved for Sadie.

There was a possibility that she could have what they call transient neonatal MG. A fancy way of saying that my antibodies (mom immunity), could have been lingering in her system for a short period of time. My immune system attacks my muscles, so of course I was worried and afraid my precious baby girl might have problems using her muscles like I did (the worst of which could be difficulty breathing or drinking a bottle). So, I decided to have them keep her in the NICU for a couple of days to monitor her closely, and they agreed this was a good idea. The first night in the NICU her heart rate randomly became elevated, and the nurses could not get it to come down. They had to start her on some medication that unfortunately we could not ween off of for 6 months. So, as you could imagine, we were a nervous wreck.

    My husband was pacing the halls of the hospital off and on all night. They had a little prayer jar at the front desk of the hospital. Once we finally were able to go home, several days later, I found about twenty of those little prayer slips in his pocket before I put them in the wash. When I asked him about it, he said he would grab a few, walk out onto the patio outside, and just pray. He never let me see his worry and fear, probably because I was already so weak, and he was just trying not to worry me. So, he brought his worry and fear to God. I know his heart was heavy, but God lightened his burden. He is literally the strongest person I know, and I am so thankful that I have a husband that loves the Lord and loves us so well.

    Worry and fear are natural responses to life's hardships. Worry reminds us that we are human, and we need God's protection. He wants us to trust Him to take care of our needs. We cannot be fearful or worrisome and trust God at the same time. It truly makes Him sad when we don't have faith in Him. Worry and fear are just as much a sin as any other. What fear and worry do you carry that you need to give to God? Spend some time in prayer laying your worries and fears at God's feet.

Ps 23 (NIV). The Lord is our protector. We lack nothing. He refreshes our soul, guides our paths, calms our fears, and comforts us. Where is your Shepard leading you? Do you trust Him? What do you need reassurance on? What fears do you need to give to God?

Jn 14:27 (NIV). God wants to give us peace. He does not want us to worry or be afraid. Pray for peace of mind and trust. Build a relationship with God! Tell God what you trust Him with!

Phil 4:6-7 (NIV). We should not be "anxious about anything." Instead, we should go to God in prayer and thanks requesting our needs. God's unexplainable peace will guard our "hearts and our minds." Name a time when you felt God's peace. Thank God for the relationship you have with Him and for His love, mercy, and provisions.

Phil 4:19 (NIV). "God will meet all your needs." Do you have faith in God to provide? Show Him that you trust Him. What is He calling you to do? Pray for God to provide a way. Then keep your eyes open because HE WILL!

Week 23: Selfishness

Giving is not easy for everyone. Servanthood is a God given gift. Some people would literally give away the shirt off their back. They would not even stop and think twice about it. I have to be honest, giving my time, money, or rest away is still to this day hard for me to do. I have to pray for God to give me a servant heart. Sometimes I feel selfish when I ask to sleep in when my husband is home and not at work. He works so hard all week, yet I still ask this of him. In my defense, he usually wakes up at six or seven in the morning and can't go back to sleep anyway. Rest really makes a huge difference where my weakness is concerned. Even if it is justified, I still feel that I am being selfish. But I have to remember, being a good wife and mother requires sacrifices of my needs sometimes. A while back, when we first started tithing, we took a step of faith. We let go of our selfishness and gave to our church cheerfully. It was such a great feeling knowing we were supporting God's mission. Giving is so rewarding.

Our time is also something that we should be conscientious about. I don't know about you, but I spend way too much time on social media and watching television. If you don't have money, time is free, and it can make a huge difference in someone's life. Sometimes it is just as simple as lending an ear to a friend that is struggling, making dinner for someone, or volunteering to serve within your church. If we choose to spend our time praying and worshiping God, what a difference it would it make in our lives and in the lives of others. Our attention should be on helping others not ourselves. Some of the most selfless, most giving people I know, grew up with very little. I truly believe that sometimes God takes away, or allows us to live life in need, to make us appreciate what we have and where we came from. When you know what it is like to be in need, you are much more willing and happier to help others who are struggling. Don't be selfish, it is not an admirable quality. Pray and ask God to take away your selfish desires and give you opportunities to give to others.

Prv 11:25 (NIV). Generosity brings prosperity. Helping others succeed should be our fuel. What is fueling you?

Mk 8:34 (NIV). We must deny ourselves in order to follow Christ. Are there things still in your life that you need to turn from doing?

Eph 5:19-21 (NIV). "Submit to one another out of reverence for Christ." What do you need to thank God for? Who do you need to show love?

Phil 2:5-8 (NIV). Let your relationships mimic the humility of Christ. Do not take advantage of others, humble yourself, be a servant, and be obedient to God even if it means persecution. Are you serving others humbly, or are you serving yourself? Are you worrying about what others think or what God thinks?

Jas 3:16 (NIV). Envy and selfish ambition lead to wickedness, and immorality. Is what you are doing furthering the Kingdom or is it contributing to the immorality of the world? Are you "standing out" for Christ or are you "blending in" for fear of dislike?

Week 24: Self-hate/ insecurities

Body image, Lack of Confidence, Poor Motivation

When we become Christians, we begin to examine ourselves. We begin to understand that we have strengths and weaknesses. One might say that it is a good idea to consider our strengths as our God given gifts. But often times, we start to notice all the areas that we need to work on in our life and fixate on them instead of our strengths. It is true that we need to try to improve and clean up our lives, but what truly matters is that we recognize our own gifts and use them so that people begin to see the outward signs of Christ in our lives. We should be confident in the image God gave us! He makes no mistake, and we are one of His beautiful creations. We should be confident using the voice God gave us to share our story. Our story matters to God, and it just might make a difference in someone else's life. There is beauty even in our brokenness.

We should also be confident in our redemption. God sent His son to die on the cross for our sins, and we should not be afraid to share that with the world! We should not let anything distract us from our God given purpose. We should keep our guard up for Satan's attempts to get in the way of God's message! Satan will try to convince us we are not good enough, that we don't deserve to be redeemed, and that we are incapable of completing what God wants us to do! These thoughts are just futile attempts to thwart us from God's work. Rebuke Satan, and praise God for giving you all the tools you need to succeed! These verses really help me when I feel the enemy is attempting to hold me back. Spend time in the Word, so that you will be prepared to defend yourself from the enemy and take a stand for Christ! Have faith in God to give you the confidence to share His love with others.

Ps 27:1-3 (NIV). We have nothing to fear. We can be confident in our salvation. God will cause our enemies to "stumble and fall." Are you confident in your walk with Christ? Who do you need to tell about Jesus? Share your faith boldly! Let people know what makes you special!

Ps 139: 13-14 (NIV). God created us. "We are fearfully and wonderfully made." God's creation is wonderful and perfect! He does not make mistakes. He wrote our story in His book before we were ever formed. How do you view yourself? How do you think God views you? Is He proud of you? Are you proud of how you are living?

Is 32:17 (NIV). The fruit of righteousness is peace. Peace gives our minds quietness, stillness, and confidence. When we have Christ in our lives and we are living for Him, we can be confident that we are pleasing Him! Peace comes from knowing that what we are doing is good! Is the way you are living pleasing to God? Are you confidently living for Christ or are you insecure because you don't know who or what you are living for? Do you have spiritual peace?

Jer 17:7 (NIV). We are blessed when we trust God and place our confidence in Him. God rewards trust. What are you confidently trusting God with? List some things you could entrust to Him. Pray over those things! Give them to God and have faith.

1 Cor 15:58 (NIV). Commit yourself to the Lord's work. Let nothing distract you, because nothing you do is futile. Everything has a purpose. What is distracting you from fulfilling God's purpose. What obstacles are in your way? Are your own insecurities hindering your progress?

Eph 2:10 (NIV). We are God's perfect creation. He determined our purpose before we were ever born. We were created to carry out His good works. What is God's purpose for your life this season? It's ok if you don't know. It's also ok to have more than one purpose or for your purpose to change over time!

Phil 1:6 (NIV). We need to be confident that God will help us fulfill our purpose. Spend time in prayer asking God to give you the strength, confidence, and the tools to complete His work. Pray for His guidance.

Phil 4:13 (NIV). "I can do all things through Him who gives me strength." What are you capable of with God's strength? How can you push through when the going gets tough? What is your plan?

Col 3:23-24 (NIV). In everything you do, give it your all, as if you are working for the Lord. His inheritance is our reward. Have you been "Giving it all you've got?" What strengths do you still have in your back pocket? God gave you a set of tools, use them to complete the task He has given you! Do not give up!

Week 25: People Pleasing

As a young child, I found myself seeking gratification from praise and trying to please people. There is nothing wrong with accepting gratification from others. However, it should not be the reason behind our actions. I learned later on in life, that it is ok to stand up for yourself and your beliefs respectfully. You can't please everyone. Just be respectful in the way you choose to defend your beliefs. Sometimes it means closing a door in your life, because the place you are in is not good for your health or spiritual walk with Christ. Make sure that your roots are planted in fertile ground. Fruit cannot be produced without a seed, good soil, and nourishment. The people we are around should be encouraging, supportive, and overall positive examples. We should not allow people to take advantage of our good, hardworking nature. We should do good things because it brings us joy when we please God. When we are doing God's will, He is proud of us. God's way of thanking us for what we do comes in the form of blessings and opportunities. If we are not focused on Him, we may miss them when they come our way!

People pleasing is not the same thing as showing hospitality or serving. We should be concerned with showing hospitality to others, because making people feel welcome and loved is part of being a Christian. Being accommodating, generous, and friendly are very flattering characteristics to have. We want others to see Christ in us! Christ made people feel welcome and not judged. He talked to people respectfully and gently, showing them that He understood, knew, and cared for them. We should care about others' needs. We should also have a servant heart, because Christ cares for us! Christ wants us to serve others, but he does not want us to act based on what other people think of us! We should show hospitality and servitude in hopes that people will want to see more of Christ! We should also obey our authorities and the law. But, if the law goes against our beliefs, we should stand for God, no matter the cost.

Mt 10:28 (NIV). People are not the enemy, Satan is. Who do you see as the enemy? How is Satan using them to get to you? Why are you letting him? Satan just wants to get in-between you. He wants your hearts to stay hardened so the opportunity to share Christ will be lost! Don't let Satan use you!

Jn 12:26 (NIV). Jesus said, "My father will honor the one who serves me." Who are you serving? Who are you trying to please? What are you spending your time and money on?

Jn 12:42- 43 (NIV). We should not fear humans more than we fear God. The Jews were afraid of acknowledging their faith because they were afraid the Pharisees would not allow them into the synagogue. Who's praise and acceptance are you seeking? Who or what are you afraid of? Pray for God to help you fully devote yourself to Him!

Acts 5:29, 32 (NIV). "We must obey God rather than human beings! God's reward for obedience is the Holy Spirit living in us! Are you wasting His gift? Are you accommodating others by refusing to profess your faith in Jesus Christ? Who are you obeying? Does their demand match God's desires? If not, then you should be questioning where your loyalty and devotion lies.

Acts 20: 24 (NIV). Our sole purpose is to share Christ with others and win people for Jesus! Unite others with Christ by demonstrating peace. Our concern for others needs to demonstrate Christ's affection. Are you doing everything in your power to win people for Jesus? Who do you need to make peace with?

1 Cor 10:33 (NIV). Whenever you are seeking to please people, do it with the intent of reaching them for Christ. Teach others by being an example of Christ. Be a servant. Who are you serving?

Gal 1:10 (NIV). If you are trying to win the approval of people, you are not serving Christ. We have to ask ourselves who are we trying to please? Whose approval are we seeking?

Col 3:22-25 (NIV). Obey your authorities, as if you were working for the Lord. By doing so you are being a servant of Christ. God's inheritance is our reward for hard work and dedication. My mother told me many times as a child, "Do it right or don't do it at all!" What assignments do you need to put more effort into? Are you giving God your all? Are you putting your best foot forward? Are you investing in God?

1 Thess 2:4 (NIV). We should not use authority, flattery, or impure motives to force people to agree, believe, or accept us. Instead, we should use sincere encouragement, comfort, and direction in hopes that they will be convicted by God to live righteously. What methods are you using to win people over? Are your methods honorable? Are your motives honorable? It is not our job to convict people. God does the conviction we are just called to lead by example! God has to extend his offer when the time is right, and the person must be willing to accept it!

Week 26: Pride

Christ loves humility and despises pride! It is ok for us to have goals and be happy when we accomplish them, but our accomplishments should not make us feel like we are "better" than others. We are not better than anyone! God loves each and every person the same. He made us all unique and special for a purpose. God gave us different gifts, and we can use them to bring peace and unity instead of create competition and conflict. Our life should be about commission, not competition.

Glory and fame are worldly, and it does not last! If we want to win favor with God, then we should humble ourselves, seek biblical wisdom, and have faith in God instead of ourselves or others! The only thing we should boast about is our weakness and our Love for Christ! Amen! God has given us everything we have! So why are we so obsessed with ourselves? We cannot accomplish anything worthy of praise without Him! The Bible says that we will be punished for our pride! It is a sin! The knowledge of this world is nothing compared to the knowledge of our creator! It is about time we start praising Him instead for this wonderful life He has given us! Read what God's Word has to say about pride and spend some time humbling yourself before Him! He is the only one worthy of our praise!

Prv 11:2 (NIV). Pride is disgraceful, humility is wise. Are you living a life of humility? List some areas you could be more humble?

Jn 5:44 (NIV). You cannot have faith in God yet seek worldly Glory. List a few of your goals. Now cvaluate those goals and determine if they will accomplish worldly glory or glory for God. Spend time in prayer for your goals to align with God's. His desires are greater than our own.

1 Cor 3:18-20 (NIV). "The wisdom of this world is foolish in God's sight." God knows our futile thoughts, so we should not boast of wisdom. Do you consider yourself wise? What is it that makes you wise? Is the wisdom of Godly origin or of the world? Are you seeking His wisdom? What are you actively doing to gain wisdom from God? Where are you gaining wisdom from?

2 Cor 12:9-10 (NIV). We should boast in our weaknesses, because Christ's power is made perfect in weakness. When we are weak His power rests on us! God uses even our weaknesses to do good. Make a list of your weaknesses. Now pray that God would use them to do good and have Faith that He will!

Week 27: Unhealthy habits

One thing all our unhealthy habits have in common is that they are of the world! You cannot love the world and also love God. Lust and pride are from the world and worldly things "pass away." The prize for loving God is eternal. Jn 2:15-17 (NIV). These things we obsess over do not promote our spiritual growth. God wants us to focus on things that will build and strengthen His eternal Kingdom. When we obsess over worldly things, it is as if we are worshiping false idols. When in reality the only idol that can bring us true happiness and contentment is God.

Alcohol, drugs, food, media, politics, all these things take our attention off God and pollute our mind and body. We are tainting our body with unimportant/unholy things, when God wants us to commit our bodies to Him as a pure "sacrifice." If we are pouring unholy things into our body then our minds will not be focused, our thoughts will not be pure, and we will not be a righteous example for others. In fact, we are in turn giving Christ and His mission a bad name. People are watching us! When we claim Christ as our savior, people should be able to see us as an example of how "Christians" should live! We should not give them a false impression.

Worldly things are tempting because they tend to make us feel "good" temporarily. But they are just that, only temporary. The satisfaction goes away, and we become stuck in a cycle of trying to satiate a hunger that worldly things can never fulfill. But

God, he offers us happiness and satisfaction that no worldly thing can offer. When the Holy Spirit is within us, there is a sense of completeness and peace that is unexplainable! What a beautiful gift God has given us! Don't give Satan a foothold! Be strong in the Lord! The Bible is a very clear warning about temptation and what God expects of us!

Rom 12:1-2 (NIV). Our bodies belong to God. What we see, hear, and do influence us and thus transform us into who we are. We should filter such things so that we are only pouring virtue into our life. Seeking to please God not ourselves, studying His Word, and allowing Him to renew our mind body and soul will give us wisdom to discern God's will for our life. What things are you pouring into your life? Do you need to empty your unnecessary container to make room for necessary things?

1 Cor 10:13 (NIV). God will not tempt you beyond what you can handle or endure. He will give you a path out of temptation! The point of temptation is for us to prove our faithfulness to God, and for us to realize we cannot endure life without Him. He wants us to recognize our need for Him and rely on Him fully. What are you being tempted with? Is it too much for you to handle alone? Is God giving you a way out? Have you accepted His help? Pray that God would carry you through and guide you down the right path! Pray for Him to send Godly people that will be supportive in your journey. Remember God is always there even when you feel alone.

1 Cor 15:33 (NIV). "Bad company corrupts good character." Who are you spending time with? Are they positive, Godly, encouraging, influences in your life? Do you need to re-evaluate those friendships? Is there someone you don't need to be hanging around? Make the cut! Set the boundaries! God will open other doors. He will send someone your way that is an encouragement and not a deterrent! You just have to free up that time and space! Make yourself available to God and unavailable to the enemy!

Eph 4:22-24, 27 (NIV). When we are saved, we put on a "new self" that is no longer concerned with our human desires, but is concerned with living righteous, holy and in likeness of God. We are re-created by God, to live like God and for God. 27 "Do not give the devil a foothold." If you give Satan an inch, he will take a mile! What are your human desires? What are God's desires? Are you living like God and for God? What desires do you need to be focusing on? Are you giving the devil a foothold over you?

Phil 4:8 (NIV). Our thoughts should be pure! What things are you thinking about? Are they pure? Rebuke the impure thoughts! Again, don't give the devil a foothold over your mind!

1 Pt 2:24 (NIV). Christ died for our sins so that we would "live for righteousness." By His blood we are healed. What are you living for? Make a list of the most important things in your life! What are your reasons for living? Are you striving for righteousness? Make a note of the things that you are living for that are not worthy of God's praise and begin to remove those things from your life. Pray for guidance regarding how to achieve righteousness.

1 Jn 1:9 (NIV). "If we confess our sins, He is faithful and just and He will forgive us." But if we deny our sins, then it is as if we are saying God is a liar and "His word is not in us." What sins do you need to confess?

1 Jn 2:15-17 (NIV). You cannot love the world and also love God. Lust and pride are from the world and worldly things "pass away." But the prize for loving God is eternal. Do you love God or the world? List some things you are doing that prove that you love God. What are some idols you need to get rid of in order to free yourself for God's service? List those things you are putting before God.

Week 28: Toxic people

"Bad company corrupts good character." 1 Cor 15:33 (NIV). I think we are all guilty of this at some point in our life. It is hard to find good friends. They are one in a million. When we are young, we are sometimes misled in our ideas of what a friend is. A true friend does not put you down or speak ill of you. They are honest with you in a way that is gentle and loving, and they are trustworthy. They look out for what is best for you, put your needs first over their own, and would never intentionally do anything to hurt you or take advantage of you. A true friend grieves when you grieve, celebrates accomplishments with you, and is there for you and supports you in times of need without expecting anything in return. A true friend is not jealous, does not boast of their greatness, and most definitely does not gossip about you or slander your name.

Now you see why genuine friends are so hard to find. But, while they are hard to find, they are also hard to keep. You see, everything a good friend does, we should reciprocate for them. My husband is my very best friend. I know he has my best interest at heart always. I can trust Him with my life. Some people boast of having many friends. To be honest, I question the integrity of those friendships. So, this is why I tell you with love and concern, choose your friends wisely! The people you choose to be in your life, or the people you choose to work for, have a huge influence on your character. We should be guarding ourselves from people who deflate our self-worth, blow out our candle, or who deter us from using our attributes for God. Choose people who accept you and your purpose and who encourage your walk with the Lord! Pray for God to give you wisdom concerning the people you have in your life. Pray for God to send people to you that will join you in your mission for Christ! Pray for God to give you courage to cut ties with people who are holding you back from fulfilling God's purpose!

Ps 37:1-3 (NIV). God wants us to have successful lives. He does not want us to be envious of those who are taking the "easier" path. The grass on the other side is not "greener." They may be on a path to destruction. We should stay the course, trust God's direction, continue to do good, and plant our seed in the "safe pasture" that God has designated for us. God gives our life sustenance! What pasture is God asking you to plant your seed in? Are you already planted there, or do you need to uproot and go where He is calling? Are you trying to plant where your "friends" are or where God wants you? Are you truly where you need to be?

Prv 13:20 (NIV). The people who are in your life have influence on your character. Choose them wisely. Are you seeking wisdom from wise council? Who are you pouring wisdom into? Both are important! Is it Godly wisdom that you are seeking or giving?

Prv 16:28 (NIV). A corrupt person seeks conflict, and gossip ruins friendships. Are you seeking conflict because you are afraid to be content? Are you talking about people behind their back to make yourself feel better? What kind of friend are you? Are you treating friends the way you want to be treated? Are you taking a stand for what is right?

Prv 22:24-25 (NIV). Being around others who are ill-tempered, have a negative mindset, or sinful habits can cause you to be tempted in their ways or behaviors. Do not make friends with these types of people who may tempt you. Bad habits are contagious! What type of people are you around in your day to day? What type of person are you? Are you a positive influence on others or negative?

Mt 7:15-20 (NIV). Beware of "false prophets," you will recognize them by their bad fruit or lack thereof. They are deceiving, and may appear to be good, but we must use prayer and discernment to determine their truthfulness. Are you quick to believe everyone or are you wisely discerning who and what to trust? It is ok to seek truth, but are you searching for discernment in the Word and through prayer? Are you taking time to process what you believe or are you jumping to conclusions without seeking God's counsel?

Eph 4:31-32 (NIV). We must rebuke all forms of evil in our life: Bad habits, bitterness, rage, anger, fighting, trash talk, slander, and hate. What forms of evil do you need to rebuke from your life? Rebuke those things!

2 Tm 3:1-7 (NIV). (vs. 1-5) "But mark this: There will be terrible times in the last days. People will be lovers of themselves, lovers of money, boastful, proud, abusive, disobedient to their parents, ungrateful, un-holy, without love, unforgiving, slanderous, without self-control, brutal, not lovers of good, treacherous, rash, conceited, lovers of pleasure rather than lovers of God, having a form of godliness but denying its power. Have nothing to do with such people." (vs 6-7) They "are swayed by all kinds of evil desires, always learning but never able to come to a knowledge of the truth." Is there someone or something you need to stop being around? Are you being a godly representative of Christ? Make a change! I promise God will reward you for being faithful!

Week 29: Old baggage

Revenge, Guilt, Judgement, Distrust:

God has given us the most perfect gift of redemption and forgiveness. All we have to do is believe that Christ died for us, confess our sins, repent, and faithfully follow where God calls. Once we have accepted God's forgiveness, the Holy Spirit lives within us and guides us. We have to listen to the Holy Spirit and the Word of God in order to produce the fruits of righteousness. Prayer is so powerful; we should pray and trust that God is already working out His perfect plan for our lives. When we are forgiven, we then have to choose to let go of our sinful past and the old baggage in our lives! We have to let go of revenge, judgements, distrust, and guilt that we are holding on to. God forgives and forgets!

Empty the junk in your life so that you can make room for God's blessings! We are given a new blank canvas, an empty house, fresh relationships, a renewed mind. It is our job to allow God to fill us with beautiful, meaningful things! God desires for us to be satisfied with our life, but He wants us to allow him to give us that fulfillment. Let go of the past, let go of your insecurities, forgive others, forgive yourself, accept the fresh start that God offers! Don't seek fulfillment in what the world has to offer, you will be disappointed every time! God wants to help us get out of the cycle of chaos! It hurts Him to see us suffering! Put your faith in Him so that He can bless you immensely! You will be surprised at the transformation God can have on your life when you allow Him to take control! Take some time to think about where you are now, and where you want to be in a year. Pray for God to help you build that firm foundation and repair the broken pieces that are causing you to crumble! Commit yourself to His purpose, wherever that may lead!

Revenge:

Prv 20:22 (NIV). Do not try to right someone else's wrongs. God will take care of their judgement. Who do you feel has wronged you in the past? Are you able to forgive them? Pray that God would help you forgive that person.

Rom 12:19 (NIV). Do not try to punish those who have harmed you. Instead kill them with kindness, "Do not be overcome by evil, but overcome evil with good." Allow God to serve justice! Justice is not ours to inflict. Who do you need to kill with kindness?

2 Cor 13:11 (NIV). Seek peace, restore, and encourage one another and by doing this you can be comforted because the "God of love and peace will be with you." Are you allowing God to give you peace regarding people who have wronged you?

1 Pt 3:9 (NIV). Bless those who do you wrong! Seek peace and keep your eyes on the prize that is eternal life with Christ. We are still blessed even if we suffer for doing what is righteous! We have no one to fear except God. Are your eyes on the prize, or on the past? Are you suffering because you are doing the right thing? Pray and thank God for the courage He has given you to look forward even though it is difficult! Be eager to do good!

Guilt:

Jn 3:17 (NIV). Jesus came to save us, not to condemn us. Have you prayed for God to save you? Have you allowed Him to forgive you? Have you forgiven your old self? Have you pivoted and started living for Jesus?

Eph 1:7 (NIV). By grace and the blood of Christ, God has offered us redemption. He has given us the power to be forgiven of our sins should we desire to know Him. Do you desire to know God? All you have to do is pray. "God, I believe you sent your son Jesus to die on the cross for my sins. I believe that He died and rose again. I know I am a sinner, and I accept your gift of forgiveness. I want you to be Lord of my life and I surrender my Life to you God. Thank you for forgiving me!" The next steps you have already read about in this study! Get your foundation right, set yourself up for success! Understand that once you accept God, He will never leave you! He is always by your side in good times and bad.

Heb 8:12 (NIV). God forgives and forgets. Did you pray the prayer for salvation? If so, God has already forgiven you! There is no one too far gone! God desires for us all to have a relationship with Him. Are you looking ahead to the future? What does that look like? Pray for God's guidance and direction in your life!

Judgement:

Mt 7:1-5, Lk 6:37 (NIV). God will judge us based on how we judge others. God does not want us to judge others. Are you judging others instead of helping them see Christ in you? Who have you wrongfully judged? Pray for forgiveness.

Jn 8:7 (NIV). No one is without sin! We should not judge others unless we have first judged ourselves. On the opposite note, we cannot be perfect, but God wants us to be the best version of ourselves. So, we should try to live righteously, according to His Word. Are you being the best version of yourself? Are you reading His Word and applying His wisdom to your life? What things need to change in order for you to make that a priority?

Distrust:

Prv 25:19 (NIV). We should not seek advice from ungodly people when we are going through a test of our faith. They cannot help us like someone who knows the Lord. Who do you go to for advice? Are you seeking advice from the wrong people? List some people that you could go to for advice or encouragement.

Mt 5:23-24 (NIV). Make right your relationships first, and then praise and worship the Lord for His faithfulness. Is there someone you cannot trust or who does not trust you? How can you help to re-build that trust with them? What is the reason for the distrust? Can you talk to them about it? Pray and ask God for the right words and actions to take.

Rom 10:10-11 (NIV). Belief in God cannot occur without faith and trust in Him! A relationship with God requires belief, along with faith and trust. They go hand in hand, belief and trust must occur simultaneously. Do you trust God? Can He trust you? Seek to build a trusting relationship with God. Have faith in Him as He does you! This is the most important relationship in your life, make it right!

Week 30: Look for Changes in Your Life!

My prayer for all of you is that you have a better understanding of the path to organizing your life the way God designed! I hope you have begun to see the transformation process and have allowed God to take control of your chaos! He is in control, we are not! Amen for that! The best, truest, and most faithful therapist is free. He does not judge, and He already knows all of our thoughts. We can come to him any time, day or night. All we have to do is ask and we will receive His help. He offers wisdom and discernment to anyone who believes in Him. He loves us unconditionally. When you develop a firm foundation, let go of control, establish self-awareness, re-organize your life priorities, and get rid of the chaos, the other areas of your life will begin to transform as well!

There are so many areas of our life that are impacted by our foundation. If we do not establish self-awareness, we don't know our strengths and weakness or how to use them! Our necessary containers must include priorities and virtues that are in line with God's. We must let Him take control. Finally, we must empty our unnecessary containers in order to get rid of the chaos it brings into our life. When we follow these steps, we will see God begin to prune our life! With dedication to our walk with God, we will begin to experience harmony, peace, health, wealth, happiness, and the list goes on. Fruitfulness is the goal! Our fruitfulness will begin to overflow into other areas of our life! With God's guidance and strength, the opportunity for growth is limitless! Let Him define who you are! When people see you and hear your story, they should see Jesus! His light should be flowing out of you!

Take Aways

1. What have you learned about your foundation? Is it weak or strong?

2. What do you need to allow God to take control of?

3. What are you more "self-aware" of now?

4. What are your strengths and weaknesses?

5. How can God use you?

6. What things do you need to prioritize in your life?

7. What is God calling you to do?

8. What is your purpose?

9. What unnecessary junk do you need to get rid of?

10. What is causing chaos in your life?

Moving Forward

Do you have other areas of your life that need organizing and prioritizing in a way that is pleasing to God? I will be focusing on how to organize these specific areas in future books in my series! I hope you truly are beginning to see how a firm foundation is the basis for a life centered around Christ. Putting Him first is crucial. With Christ as our foundation, we can be stronger than the storms! Let's rebuild our lives, one area at a time, with God's direction and guidance! Use this list to help you identify needs for transformation. List specific things that could use re-organizing!

Relationships:

Finances:

Homelife:

Health/ selfcare:

Family life/ time:

Career:

Acknowledgements

To my husband Will Newman for always being supportive and reminding me who is in control, God. Thank you for always loving me, encouraging me to stand up for myself, and most importantly giving me a reason to not give up daily. Thank you for your unwavering love and faith. There is no one else that I would rather experience life with. There is no doubt that God handpicked you for me. I love you more than words.

To my mother Vicki Bland, who fought for me when no one else would. You are the bravest, strongest, most selfless person I know, and my number one supporter. You are such a Godly inspiration to me and so many others. I can never repay you enough for all your sacrifices. I love you Mom. And to My father Steve Bland, who is always there whenever I need anything without complaint! He has always made my dreams come true! I love you Dad!

To my sister Faith Austin and Brother-in-Law Michael Austin, thank you for always being supportive, and for being such great role models for your niece! I look forward to repaying the favor one day soon! I love you both!

To the doctors and nurses that have cared for me over the years, specifically Kenneth D. Groshart MD, Tulio E. Bertorini MD, and Louise Matthews RN. (To many more not mentioned, but all so appreciated). You have all selflessly taken care of me and have always been in my corner since my diagnosis. For that I will be forever grateful! I would not be alive today if it were not for your love and commitment and for God's hand of protection. You have all gone above and beyond your oath of practice. Thank you, from the bottom of my heart, may God reward you for your dedication

References

Michelle, LaKeisha. 2023, May 20. Influence Surge, Nashville TN.

Scripture quotations taken from The Holy Bible, New International Version ® NIV ® Copyright ©1973, 1978, 1984, 2011 by Biblica, Inc.™ Used by permission. All rights reserved worldwide.

Some content taken from (Pleasures Evermore: The Life Changing Power of Knowing God) by (Sam Storms). Copyright © (2000). Used by permission of NavPress, represented by Tyndale House Publishers. All rights reserved.

West, M. 2023, February 17. My Story Your Glory. Copyright Provident Music Group ©

Organizing Your Life God's Way: From Chaos to Control

This book series is designed to help you organize your life in the way God designed. He wants to transform our lives from chaos to control, but we have to allow Him to clean up our mess! God has given us all a special purpose and he will give us the strength and tools we need to fulfill it! Join me on a journey to get our lives back on track for God's mission! Starting with our foundation first, we will be able to set ourselves up for success in all other areas of our life! The goal of this series is to help us successfully build or rebuild our home-life, relationships, career, health/lifestyle, and finances in a way that pleases God! Allow God to help you reorganize your life on a firm foundation of Biblical knowledge and wisdom, so that you can understand and fulfill your God given purpose!!

Future Books in this Series

Prioritized Relationships

Organized Homelife

Disciplined Finances

Effective Self Care

Purposeful Family Time

Calling-Led Career

Follow the Author: Social Media Profiles

Facebook: Organize Your Life for God

Twitter: @KNewmanWrites

Instagram: KNewmanWrites

Email: AuthorKelliNewman@gmail.com

www.ingramcontent.com/pod-product-compliance
Lightning Source LLC
Chambersburg PA
CBHW081204170426
43197CB00018B/2915